About the Author

Bruno Gideon is a highly regarded businessman and author, an entrepreneur with many years of hands-on experience in Italy, France, England, and in his native country, Switzerland. He envisioned and built three multi-million-dollar corporations from the ground up, all in fiercely competitive markets.

Bruno is fascinated by the way people communicate, whether under tough business conditions or in day-to-day life. He strongly believes that the key factor for success is the ability to convince others on a give-and-take basis, and he lives by this principle.

As a journalist and author, Bruno for many years had a column in major newspapers and wrote seven books that made him a best-selling author in German-speaking Europe. His book *Don't Take No for an Answer!* has in particular received high critical praise.

Bruno has a unique writing style. He is an expert in breaking complex matters into smaller components. His books are filled with everyday examples, making them easy to read and very understandable.

Today, Bruno is a Canadian citizen living in Toronto. His passions, aside from writing, are his dogs and dog shows.

If you would like to learn more about Bruno, go to:

www.brunogideon.com

Bruno Gideon

Don't Take No for an Answer!

5 Proven Steps
That Get You to Yes

**A Guide for Exceptional Success
in Business and Everyday Life**

MATTERHORN
PUBLISHING

First published in 2003 by
Matterhorn Publishing Inc.
20 Elm Avenue
Toronto, Ontario M4W 1N3

www.brunogideon.com

To order Matterhorn books please contact
Hushion House Publishing Limited
36 Northline Road
Toronto, Ontario M4B 3E2
Telephone 416-285-6100
Fax 416-285-1777

National Library of Canada Cataloguing in Publication Data

Gideon, Bruno, 2003

Don't Take No for an Answer! 5 Proven Steps that Get You to Yes.

ISBN 0-9732491-1-0 (trade paperback)

1. Business   2. Self Help

This book is available at special discounts for bulk purchases by groups or
organizations for sales promotions, premiums, fundraising, and
seminars. For details contact Matterhorn Publishing Inc., Special Sales
Department, 20 Elm Avenue, Toronto, Ontario M4W 1N3
Telephone 416-966-0036 / Fax 416-920-2962
or the author at **info@brunogideon.com**

Consultant: Arnold Gosewich
Editor: Donald G. Bastian
Book Design: Fortunato Design Inc.
Cover Photograph: V. Tony Hauser

Printed and bound in Canada

I dedicate this book to my
negotiating partners over many years,
especially the ones who beat me.

Thank you for giving me
the opportunity to learn.

Contents

STEP FIVE / Don't Take No for an Answer!

AND KEEP IN MIND

Foreword

How Bruno gets to yes

What might have happened if I had read this book more than 30 years ago? Would my life have taken a different course? These are rhetorical questions, for no one reads a book the night before her wedding!

You see, I am married to the man who reveals in this book how he (almost always) succeeds in getting his own way, without causing hurt. And I can confirm that in fact he mostly does just that, not only in business dealings, but also in his private life. The past years have not always been completely painless, but we remain a good team to this very day.

Friends, acquaintances, and strangers ask me, "How can you stay by the side of a man who not only knows how to get his own way, but even wrote a book about it?" Let me tell you the story of our dog, Shiva.

I am fond of animals, but many years ago I was against the idea of having a dog. The daily duty of taking it out for walks, the problem of what to do when going on vacation, dog hair all over the carpets and furniture... Bruno listened calmly to my objections and said nothing. Every now and then he gently revisited the subject of a dog: how much safer I would feel with this animal about, how going for walks in all kinds of weather is good for one's health, and so on.

We never quarreled about it, he simply kept returning again and again to the subject. He had probably noticed my opposition was not as total as I pretended. And then it happened. I heard by chance about a dog needing a new home. To this very day I don't know why I told my husband. All Bruno said was we could take a look at the dog without committing ourselves. And that was my undoing.

Shiva, a golden retriever, laid her head on my lap and looked up at me with her deep, melting brown eyes. Only someone with a heart of stone could have refused after that!

Even for my husband, things did not always go his way. When we got married I worked as a secretary and Bruno earned his living as a buyer for a food store. There was a reorganization at his firm and when we returned from our honeymoon, a blue envelope lay in our mail box – Bruno's services were no longer required.

This news hit him hard, but in hindsight we can see it paved the way to his success. Against strong opposition from established traders, he built the first cash-and-carry chain in Switzerland; in 1968 we jointly founded the first independent discount grocery chain, Pick and Pay. Now it was even more important than before to get what we wanted; it became a matter of survival, because the more success we had the more obstacles our competitors put in our path.

I will never forget the opening of our first Pick and Pay store. We lugged boxes about, filled shelves, wrote out prices, sat at the cash desk, and bought goods. Or rather, Bruno bought the goods. Our "office" was limited to a few square yards of floor space. It was there we met with the sales representatives. I often left this little space, not only because it was too crowded, but also because I could not bear hearing the continual haggling over the best price.

I felt sorry for those who were up against my husband: I knew his aim – buying at the cheapest price – was important for a discount grocery enterprise, and he always was up to the challenge. He was at his best when up against a partner of equal ability. He juggled factual arguments, appealed to the other person's feelings, brought his immense charm into play after initially presenting a tough front, and pulled out all the stops until he got what he wanted.

I usually felt badly for the poor sales reps, but it became clear that they also enjoyed the game. What a disappointment to both of them to come to a premature agreement, a slightly unbalanced compromise! Where was the fun in that? I noticed that in the best deals the winner always aimed at flexible goals: a discount, for example, didn't have to be exactly six percent, but rather between four and eight percent.

That must have been when the idea of writing this book was born. We often discussed how little is achieved in transactions through direct force, but that, all the same, there was no reason not to drive a hard bargain right to the limit. The real skill comes into play in defining the limit of what you will pay and, above all, the limits of your partner. (Always leave your opponents a chance to save face, especially if they have been forced to give in.)

What about you? Getting the right information, investigating motives, asking the right questions and giving the right answers, listening actively, and taking no to mean what in most cases it really does mean: "Maybe yes, but not right at this moment or perhaps in a slightly different way" – all these tactics will lead you to getting your own way.

Best of luck to you, dear reader!

LUCIE GIDEON

Don't Take No for an Answer!

Introduction

We all know people who achieve nearly all their goals, who succeed at almost everything they do, who get whatever they want, apparently without effort. How do they do it? Do they have special abilities the rest of us just don't possess? Are they gifted, extraordinary people? No! They are ordinary people like you and me. They just know how to get what they want. They don't take no for an answer.

All of us can learn how to get what we want, whether in business, at home, or in our leisure pursuits. The key is communication, and this book is your ticket to reaching your goals through communicating successfully. The information set out in this book is about getting to yes by taking five proven steps that together make up one powerful communications strategy, whether you are dealing with business partners, competitors, family members, or friends, and whether the communications vehicle is conversation, discussion, or negotiation.

These insights can be applied generally, for both business and personal benefit, and are laid out so every reader can easily profit from them. Each chapter is self-contained so it can be worked through on its own; each step is designed to lead you to better results. The methods portrayed are drawn directly from practical experience and real life, where they have been used to great success.

But I hear your objection: Isn't insisting on getting our own way selfish and immature? Yes, it can be, but when people work hard to get their way while respecting the existence and rights of others, good things begin to happen for everyone. The whole level of social discourse rises. In fact, getting your own way is a creative process calling for new ideas and new, unconventional ways of thinking. Remember that someone "losing" to someone who has mastered this process is learning; their own game is being elevated!

Many of my own experiences over the years inform the advice in this book. My business career really started when I was 28 years old. I was fired from my job as a buyer for a food store because of a reorganization. In hindsight, this turned out to be a stroke of luck. I took away with me an idea for a wholesale self-service market for retailers, which didn't exist then in Switzerland. Problem was, I had no money to realize this idea myself. So I came up with a business plan and submitted it to a large company. They trusted me, and within seven years I had built the Cash and Carry chain, which turned out to be a cash cow for them.

At the age of 35 I decided to go into business for myself in order to put together an idea that I had been playing with for a long time: opening a discount food store. I handed in my resignation, applied for a loan from the bank, and six months later opened my first store, under the name Pick and Pay. Over the years, together with my wife, I developed this company into a chain of 20 stores with yearly revenues of $120 million – and then sold it.

Why did I sell? Because the work had become routine. It

was not exciting anymore. And another idea kept creeping into my head: computers. The computer age had just started, and I was excited by the potential. My next move was to open the first computer store in Switzerland, to which I gave the name Microspot. This also developed into a chain of stores. It still exists today, and so do the other companies I founded.

After selling Microspot, I was financially independent and able to fulfill a lifelong dream: writing. I wrote a weekly column about finances in two Swiss newspapers and had my own column in a Sunday paper. I also appeared on a phone-in TV show and acted as a business consultant. Then I started writing books – seven of them so far, all of them selling well.

In all of these efforts I learned again and again that succeeding in business and in personal life depended on applying the five steps to getting to yes which I describe in this book.

How to get the most from this book

Read it through and then leaf through it again. Are there passages or examples that seem particularly apt? What amazed or annoyed you? Some chapters may have subject matter that is particularly relevant to your situation. Begin your training with these. You will be most motivated to read these chapters, and they will help you get the fastest results. Apply what you learn here, step by step, to everyday life and read other books on the subject.

You will find that learning to get your own way is similar to learning a foreign language. Confidence comes through constant practice. Success will come relatively quickly and you will soon be able to put your new skills to the test. Very soon you will steer your way subtly and gracefully through communications challenges. You will develop a different attitude toward problems in general and discover new methods of solving them. Perhaps that is all you are looking for. But if you want to go further and strive for greater heights of perfection, three things are important: practice, practice, and practice.

Two frogs fell into a tin full of cream. The first frog shouted, Help! I'm drowning! And eventually he did. But the second frog "didn't take no for an answer." He kicked wildly and finally, weary but triumphant, escaped by leaping from the top of a mountain of butter!

I hope you use your newly acquired talent carefully, responsibly, and in moderation. Applied in this way, the methods of this book will help you set the right atmosphere for communication and negotiation that will make you a winner.

Setting
the Stage

Chapter 1

Winners know how to lose

We must discuss three very important matters before exploring the five powerful steps to getting what you want. This chapter deals with questions that will help you develop the right attitude for successful communication and negotiation. Chapter 2 advises you on the attitude toward other people that paves the way to success. And Chapter 3 stresses how you're halfway there when you create the right atmosphere.

Allow me to ask you six questions:

- ❏ **Are you a good loser?**

- ❏ **Can you learn from your mistakes?**

- ❏ **Can you free yourself from constant self-criticism?**

- ❏ **Are you a long-term planner?**

- ❏ **Are you aware that today's losers may be tomorrow's winners?**

- ❏ **Do you take everything personally?**

Question #1
Are you a good loser?

"You can't win 'em all" is a familiar phrase. No one can win each and every time. It would be nice, but it's not going to happen. Instead, we need to look at succeeding not as a skill to be tackled in a pig-headed way, but as the capacity to take two steps forward and one step back. Anyone can win; it takes more skill and discipline to be a good loser.

Look at the world of sports. When we see the swimmer receiving his medal or the tennis champion raising her trophy, we tend to forget that the road to their goals was paved with countless defeats: setbacks caused by their own bodies, by the competition, by envy, injustice, or resentment. Only someone able to surmount every single one of these obstacles can finally come through as a winner. This is why the ability to lose gracefully is an attribute of winning. Only those who know how to lose can succeed in getting their own way.

We must embrace this attitude wholeheartedly as it ensures our flexibility. And flexibility, as we shall see, is a powerful attribute.

What is required is the ability to give in when appropriate. Often it is wiser and more economical to give in, to go back a step and gather new strength, than to continue a senseless negotiation. The person winning the discussion, if a true champion, will allow the loser a chance to back down gracefully and save face.

Let me run another idea by you about winning. As important as winning is to us, it's just as important to our opponent.

This reminds me of something my 12-year-old nephew said while watching me play with our dog, Shiva. He intuitively grasped the business of winning and losing, calling to me, "Please let Shiva win sometimes, too!"

We should consider letting our opponent win in certain situations, as long as it doesn't endanger our long-term goals. This lets us be good losers and can create goodwill. (See Question #5 for more on this.)

There are, however, two valid reasons for asserting your wishes and not giving in, even in unimportant matters.

(a) If it concerns your self-esteem. Your self-esteem must be preserved at all costs. You must avoid being set up as a paper tiger. However, even in this situation, refrain from railroading people. There are always other ways.

(b) If it brings you closer to your main goal. Often it is necessary to set the ground rules to establish your credibility, which means it can be worthwhile getting your way even on unimportant issues. This can smooth the way when it comes to bigger problems. However, even here, if you should experience a situation where you cannot win an argument, be a good loser and don't forget that you'll almost always get a second chance.

Question #2
Can you learn from your own mistakes?

You usually get a second chance to correct a problem or get a better deal, but only if you recognize and learn what went wrong. Here's an example from my own life many years ago.

> *I was working as a clerical assistant at the reception desk of a downtown hotel, when a well-known businessman offered me the position of chief buyer in his chain of restaurants. I accepted at once as this was the opportunity I had longed for. The employer promised to get in touch with me about my salary. I remember his call well; it came at the very busiest time of day on the desk; countless guests were milling about, all wanting to be served at*

once. My future employer offered me a meager salary. Worried about serving the many guests, I quickly agreed and went back to work. A short time later in a quiet moment to myself, I realized what absurd terms I had accepted. My anger came too late; I had given my word. It took me one full year to make up for my mistake.

Now I have a personal policy on this. Whenever I'm too busy to give a phone call my full attention, or allot it an adequate amount of time, I automatically reply in a non-committal way: "May I call you back?" "Can I get back to you tomorrow?" or "How long will you be in the office?" This provides me with time to think and has more than made up for what that year cost me. Some of our worst mistakes are made when we feel we have to make decisions on the spot. It is always preferable to turn the situation around so that time is on your side.

Question #3
Can you free yourself from constant self-criticism?

Once you establish that one of your decisions was wrong, don't waste energy on self-reproach or sink into a torment of self-recrimination. Instead, concentrate on doing these three things:

❏ Limit the damage

❏ Try again (don't take no for an answer)

❏ Analyze the mistake you made and remember that you have learned a lesson

When you have recovered from the pressure of the situation and the pain of the disappointment, you should make another attempt by an alternative route. (See Chapter 13, No Means Maybe.)

Question #4
Are you a long-term planner?

There is a vast difference between short-term and long-term planning. Short-term planning leads you to aim for immediate success. Long-term planning helps you concentrate on a chain of events all directed toward a final goal. Whether you win or lose along the way is irrelevant as long as you are moving in the right direction and are not losing sight of your ultimate goal. Defeats along the way often turn out to be blessings in disguise.

Question #5
Are you aware that today's losers may be tomorrow's winners?

If a business partner tells you up front that she is going to do everything she can to convince you of something, right away you will get your back up. You probably will attempt to argue every point. And so you should remember that revealing your intentions too soon is unwise, making it difficult, if not impossible, to get what you want. For every move there is a counter-move, so leave your opponent in the dark about your own goals until the matter has been settled. Even then you should resist the urge to flaunt a brilliant strategy that resulted in victory. Understandably, you will want to pat yourself on the back. However, trust me, if you show your cards now, you will give away your intentions, and you will pay for it the next time around.

Remember that current negotiations can prepare the ground for the next round. I have made it a habit to thank those I have negotiated with, particularly if the deal has gone in my favor. This may seem somewhat unusual and must be done carefully – you don't want your partner to think you are secretly making fun of him. By not savoring my current triumph at the cost of my opponent, I can smooth the ground just a little in readiness for the next time.

It certainly is wrong to gloat over your victory and brand the other person a loser. Nobody likes that; no one wants to offer himself up for sacrifice. Even if you never expect to run into the other person again, avoid gloating! Rejoicing in the wrong place at the wrong time can cost you dearly. Keep in mind that a magician never shows how he does his tricks. If he did, all the magic would vanish.

Question #6
Do you take everything personally?

We often take things personally, even if they are voiced without any accusation or are just harmless remarks. When we do receive unasked for criticism, that makes matters even worse. Defensiveness is damaging, because it clouds our judgment. We feel attacked and the automatic "fight or flight" reaction takes over. When we are in this mode we make decisions that are not rational. Both fight and flight are equally wrong, because the solution of the problem lies within us. We should refrain from any immediate reaction and ask ourselves whether we are absolutely sure that it was an attack. If we are honest, we'll see that in most cases, the other person's statement was harmless.

Denise, a friend of mine, has many positive qualities. She is nice, warm-hearted, and helpful to other people. And she is good looking. But she has a major weakness: she always arrives extremely late to any meeting, and that is very aggravating to anyone involved. If we agreed on lunch for 12 noon, she would be there at 1.

She was always the last to arrive at a party.

How would you react to such a situation? Here's how people reacted to her: some became angry and would not invite her back. Others severed their ties with her or decreased their communication.

All of them took Denise's lateness personally, but of course Denise did not mean it personally. Whatever she was trying to prove with her lateness was her own problem and was not directed to other people. She was not late in order to punish others; her lateness was part of her personality and probably only a psychologist could help her. I tried many times, but to no avail.

What reaction would be in synch with this book? First, you would have to ask yourself if the friendship with Denise was important to you. Second, whether you could accept her lateness, realizing there is nothing you can do about it and that it is not directed toward you. If you can answer yes to both questions, you very well could save a friendship.

I decided to answer yes to both questions. When I have a meeting with Denise now, I always take a book with me and read while I wait. And you know what? Suddenly she is on time to all our meetings!

Summing up

Be a good loser because today's loser often is tomorrow's winner. It is equally important to be self-critical and to learn from your mistakes, but there is no need to overdo it. Don't waste energy of self-reproach or sink into a torment of self-recrimination. Learn your lesson and move on. And don't take everything personally.

Chapter 2

Winners take others seriously

However you go about getting your own way, the person you are negotiating or communicating with is never an anonymous organization, bureaucracy, or corporation. He is always a human being. It may well be that he takes strength from representing a big organization, but he is still made of flesh and blood, with all the joys and cares, hopes and fears, abilities and inhibitions of the human race.

Unless you can create a good working relationship with this human being, you will never get anywhere. Keeping a positive attitude throughout negotiation or in any type of communication is one of the rules of getting your own way. You will not get your way by going up against the will of the other person; you must use persuasion. Nothing will work unless you are working with the other as you move toward an ultimate goal. You must be well-disposed – or at least neutral – toward the other.

To establish a starting point for neutral negotiation and persuasion, you must respect the other and be open to differing points of view. Quite rightly, your opponent expects you to take his point of view seriously, even if it is diametrically opposed to your own. The less you agree with his point of view, the more you should try to understand it. To understand does not mean to accept but to come to know the other's position; to really listen to the other person. It is a question of tolerance, of whether there is room for another point of view alongside your own.

It is important to foster an attitude toward the other person's viewpoints that combines genuine interest, an honest attempt at understanding, and a presumption of worthiness. Every word, every gesture, every look (even if unconscious) directly influences the quality of your future relationship.

The more strongly you reject the other's
point of view, the faster misunderstandings
and obstacles will pile up.

A sudden build-up of misunderstandings should set off alarm bells. This build-up often indicates tension and conflict lurking just under the surface. Keep a constant check on your feelings to see whether areas of conflict are forming up. Devote yourself immediately to whatever is causing the problem. Try to improve the atmosphere. Only then should you carry on with further negotiation. Problems are immeasurably easier to solve when the human elements are in order. When you listen to each other and try to understand each other, misunderstandings can be avoided or eliminated. (More on this theme in Chapter 3, Winners Create a Good Atmosphere.)

Watch what you say

Have you ever been offended by a harmless remark made in passing, even though it was not meant personally? This can happen to all of us, so be careful what you say to your partner in negotiation.

A very large woman I knew continually joked about her weight. It seemed as if she was encouraging others to make just as disrespectful remarks about her weight problem, but of course no one did. That is, until one day, when a friend took her up on it and playfully asked, "How many tons did you say you'd lost already?" Although this friend was only repeating in other words the sentiments continually expressed by the woman herself, a lasting animosity was immediately created between them.

Keep a close watch on your mouth. For instance, think about how hurtful it would be if someone in a group of people made disparaging comments about smoking, never thinking that one of those present was a heavy smoker who could not control his addiction.

You can be too nice, though. Sometimes it is easier to pay someone a compliment than to be honest, but sooner or later people will find you out. Here is an example from the world of dog shows, one of my hobbies.

I know a dog-show judge, a very nice woman who is highly esteemed in that world. Let's call her Paula. When someone shows her a dog and wants her opinion, she always finds nice words, complimenting the owner on the dog's beauty and gait. Paula is too nice to say a critical word – I have never heard her say anything negative to anyone. But there is a downside. When she does her work – and she is a thorough and honest judge – she sometimes has to disqualify the very dog she has praised, which angers the owner of the dog. Paula pays a price for always being nice.

When you do speak frankly, you must still consider the feelings of others. This will help to eliminate misunderstandings and keep a neutral negotiating atmosphere. Try to put yourself in the other person's shoes.

Giving due praise

Who are your best friends? What do you have in common? Even though we haven't met, I am sure your friends show you that they like you. We really like people who like us and who show it. We also must show people we like them, working on this aspect of friendship. The same is true in business. We enjoy doing business with people we like: people who show us they like us and who treat us with respect.

> *I know a businessman who is held in high esteem in all social circles; some people's admiration borders on worship. He consistently praises every good thought, intention, and deed of his colleaques and friends, while still maintaininq his credibility. I don't know whether his reasons for doing so are calculating, but I doubt that they are. He just thinks positively. If someone complains about the wet weather, he remarks on how the fields benefit from rain. He once even said, "If your wife comes home with a dented car, how do you know she wasn't out buying you a present?"*

This reminds me of an incident from my own life.

> *Once I borrowed my parents' car and brought it home badly damaged by a hit-and-run driver. Although the accident wasn't my fault, I was most reluctant to tell my parents. My father looked at the damage, asked how it happened, and just spoke one sentence: "Don't worry about it – it wasn't your fault and we need a new car anyway." That positive response took away my feelings of guilt and was an immense help to me as I matured.*

Think about nature. The interdependent life of plants and

animals is not based on competition, as Darwin thought, but on harmony. Even predators ensure that their prey continues to flourish (as a species, of course, not as individuals). This observation taken from the animal kingdom can also be applied to a human context. Those who begrudge everything, who set traps instead of forging bonds, might very well have temporary success, but they will scarcely be able to enjoy it properly if they are always watching over their shoulders. And they will never understand the skill of subtly getting their own way. There is a popular saying that aptly encapsulates this truth: "He who sets traps for others will fall in one himself."

Eric was a personal trainer in a fitness club. He was not well liked by his colleagues because he displayed an air of arrogance and never socialized with them. But his results were outstanding, and he managed to book more personal-training sessions than any other trainer.

One day, to everyone's surprise, he was promoted to be the new manager of the club. But this promotion did not sit well with the staff. Two trainers decided to leave the club because they did not want to work under Eric. However, while handing in their resignations, they had a frank and personal discussion with Eric, feeling they had nothing to lose. They told him in no uncertain terms the general opinion in which he was held.

Eric was shocked. He started asking questions and ended up discussing his situation with the two trainers for over two hours. He thanked them for their honesty and persuaded them to stay and give him a chance.

Eric did in fact change his attitude. He became more sociable. He took his trainers' needs seriously. Today he is well liked and is doing an outstanding job. I know, because I am a member of his club and had the opportunity to witness this remarkable transformation.

This example shows the power of taking others seriously and learning from mistakes. The honesty of the trainers represents the other side of the coin of giving praise where it is due. Sometimes frankness is what is required. It can have a powerful effect. People are more willing to change than we think.

Summing up

In this chapter, I have underscored the significance of interpersonal relationships. It is important to be clear that we are working with human beings, not organizations or hierarchies. We need to think before we speak, so as to not hurt the other person. We should give honest praise where praise is due, to superiors as much as to subordinates.

Chapter 3

Winners create a good atmosphere

Besides knowing how to lose and how to take others seriously, winners know how to create a good atmosphere.

No matter how strong your position and how well thought-out your arguments, if the working atmosphere is not favorable you will have difficulty getting what you want. Just as a strong headwind holds a cyclist back, so a bad atmosphere puts a drag on successful negotiation. A good or at least neutral environment is an important prerequisite for success. It is important, therefore, to avoid or defuse resistance.

If the relationship sours for any reason, whether because of one party's bad behavior or because of events in the past, you must first try to improve it before settling down to the real business of achieving your aims.

Avoiding conflict

We must attempt to create a favorable working relationship by building rapport, thus preventing a bad atmosphere from developing in the first place. In ancient times, speakers would introduce themselves to the public and, at the very start of their speech, try to win the favor of the audience by feigning modesty or flattering them. Nowadays, such false humility is seldom encountered because it is a transparent tactic.

It is important not to go too far; the balance between understatement and overstatement is wafer-thin. Small gestures are sometimes enough. A letter of sympathy or congratulations, a little birthday surprise, perhaps a telephone call or another token of friendship can often create goodwill. It is not the gift itself that is important, but the unspoken message: "I like you and care about your friendship or business relationship."

A few examples

At a class reunion, the most successful student is invited to make the welcoming speech. His career has raised his status far above that of his schoolmates. He begins with the following words:

> *"It is good to see so many familiar faces again. Looking back now I can see how our shared experiences helped to shape my life and I feel truly lucky to have known you..."*

His words had only one purpose: to make his listeners feel good and to prepare them for what was to come. The speaker went on to conduct a successful fundraiser for a child.

A singer on stage might say at some point:

> *"You're a wonderful audience! This has been a great night! I look forward to returning to your beautiful city again and again!"*

The audience greets this with affection, even given its obvious insincerity. Everyone knows she says this at every tour stop. Tolerance of this type of statement is much higher with performers than in private life or business because the audience is caught up in the moment.

Capturing goodwill is not enough; it only enables you to make a good start and forms an initial bond. But be aware that you're treading on very thin ice. You can reach surer ground only if you succeed in establishing a genuine partnership.

Establishing genuine partnerships

Meeting new people is one of the biggest challenges we face. Starting conversations with strangers and trying to make them meaningful, especially in a business situation, will be easier if you use the following suggestions.

When meeting people for the first time, concentrate on things you have in common: the same line of business, children of the same age, enjoyment of the same sports activities, pursuit of the same hobbies. Remaining personal and friendly while avoiding divisive issues helps establish good connections. Talk to the other person often and ask questions to find out what interests her. I cannot stress enough the importance of active listening.

The trick to creating partnerships is to avoid the useless small talk that unfortunately has become an integral part of getting to know each other. Chit-chat about the weather, politics, or the neighbors may help to overcome insecurity, but it forges few real bonds. Partnership, on the other hand, depends on paying attention and listening, on becoming involved and interested in the other person. As you get to know people and notice something you like about them, a new ring, a special tie, a new haircut, or perhaps a particularly happy facial expression, be sure to mention it. You will be pleasantly surprised by their reactions.

By the way, if you have a good memory, you are at a distinct advantage. You can bring up topics that others have long forgotten. (See more in Chapter 10, The Art of Speaking.)

Don't avoid dangerous subjects

We often shy away from bringing up what we consider to be taboo subjects but which in fact may be of great importance to the person we are talking to. Disabled people unfortunately have to put up with many unpleasant experiences in this regard. Don't avoid tackling dangerous subjects, for example the death of a person close to one of you, an accident, a separation, a defamatory newspaper article, the loss of a job, and so on.

Recently I met an acquaintance I hadn't seen for several months. His whole face was covered in ugly brown spots. I spoke to him very sympathetically about it and learned that he had developed them as a psychological reaction to the death of someone very close to him. Most people he met chatted to him about every subject under the sun, with the exception of his face. Everyone must have noticed the spots, but very few had the courage to inquire. The rest were afraid of broaching a taboo topic and frantically sought other subjects to discuss. As a result, he was not able to talk about his problem with anyone and receive support. He interpreted their shyness as rejection. When I mentioned the matter, the floodgates opened. At last he had an opportunity to express his feelings.

This is an example of genuine partnership established through empathy. But take care! Approach these subjects with the utmost sensitivity, wording your opening remarks so that the other person can extricate himself without seeming rude. If the person prefers not to talk about it, he will certainly let you know and clearly he is within his rights to do so. Do not take this as rejection.

Here are a few possible introductions for dealing with taboo subjects.

Someone close to your friend has died

Don't say: "I want to offer my sympathy for the loss of your husband. What exactly did he die of?"

But rather: "I want to offer my sympathy for the loss of your husband. This must be a difficult time for you." (Pause)

You have read a defamatory newspaper article about your acquaintance

Don't say: "That's some story they printed about you."

But rather: "Did you manage to refute the article in the newspaper?"

The person you're talking to has recently lost her job

Don't say: "I hear you're unemployed. What are you doing all day long?"

But rather: "Is there anything I can do to help with your job search?" (Only if you really are willing and in a position to help. Otherwise this would be a meaningless gesture.)

Friendship thrives on small gifts

I am not suggesting that you try to buy friendship. Any attempt to do so is transparent and will be unsuccessful in the long run. Such gestures should not be overdone; they are merely meant to convey, discreetly and indirectly, that you think well of the recipient. A short telephone call on a friend's birthday or a little souvenir brought back from a holiday. A short note on happy or sad occasions, a bunch of flowers to say thank you for an invitation – there are many possibilities.

Dale Carnegie, author of the classic book *How to Win Friends and Influence People*, wrote of how he would take note of his acquaintances' birthdays so he could surprise them with a birthday card. When he first met someone, he brought the conversation around to astrology so as to casually find out their birthday. He committed the date to memory and wrote it down at his first opportunity. I do the same.

I know a businesswoman who has the idea of these little sweeteners down to a fine art. Not only does she have an instinct for the right balance between too much and too little, she also has a creative streak when it comes to choosing these personal gifts. I asked her how she manages to be attentive to so many people despite the demands of her job. She answered, "My secretary and my computer."

Perhaps this seems a bit matter-of-fact, but it doesn't matter how you organize things. Using the computer as a memory-aid and delegating to her secretary what it reminds her to do enables this businesswoman to spread a bit of good cheer and promote good relationships.

The other side of the coin

These little gestures are one side of the coin. Sooner or later you will stumble onto the other: indifference. If your well-meant gesture sinks without a trace and no thanks are sent, how do you find out whether the intended recipient got the flowers, chocolates, or birthday card?

It is natural, of course, to feel angry about an unacknowl-edged gift. I have even been so carried away by my annoyance at apparent ingratitude that I made the shop ask whether the recipient received my gift, and I initiated a search for a parcel at the post office. After some time, this usually elicits a somewhat forced thank-you note, which causes awkwardness all around.

If the person neglects to thank you on an isolated occasion, it might be a misunderstanding or forgetfulness. But if you are really upset, the direct method is the best. Take the earliest opportunity to get the problem out of the way by asking without beating around the bush whether the present arrived. If this situation happens repeatedly with different people, you should examine your approach critically. Be honest with yourself and ask yourself a few questions:

❑ Have I overdone it?

❑ What was my real motive?

❑ Did I really want to please or was I only after gratitude?

❑ Is this the first time with this person that no acknowledgment was forthcoming?

Your responses to these and similar questions will help you to see things clearly. Just keep in mind that there are some people who never say thank you or only after months have passed. If that happens to me repeatedly, I take it as a sign that my attentions are unwanted and I put an end to them.

Playing fair: dealing with divisive factors

Disputes of many kinds can arise in relationships, whether quarrels, arguments, differences of opinion, or other problems. With emotions running high it can be difficult to focus on getting what you want and even harder to do it without hurting anyone. Such situations need to be cleared up quickly and objectively. The more difficult your position is, the more objective you must become. The relationship is no longer the priority; setting the situation right is.

*Never let yourself be provoked and at all costs
keep your temper under control!*

Make an effort to be objective and concentrate on solving the problem. Accept accusations, justifications, or corrections, but don't get more involved emotionally than you have to. Your priority should be the elimination of the basic problem. Avoid taking positions of attack or defense and ignore attempts to saddle you with feelings of guilt. Remember to use the word "fair." An appeal to the person's sense of fairness often works wonders. At all costs prevent the discussion from revolving around the questions "Who is to blame?" and "Whose fault is it?" This can only lead to disappointment.

Example taken from the building industry
A negative approach:

A: I have been waiting for you to fix these windows for three weeks now and the job still hasn't been done. I called you so many times and you promised to come but nothing happens. I can tell you that I'm getting really angry.

B: We had to finish a big job before the weather changed and I had two men call in sick and just couldn't do it. But I'll come next week and fix it, if that is okay with you.

A: Promises, promises. You have lost all credibility. I want the windows fixed by this Friday or I'll call my lawyer and sue.

B: I'll try, but I can't promise. I am sorry, but...

A: Walks away...

Comment: If A wants to have his windows fixed on time, he is using the wrong approach. He is doing much harm with his uncontrolled anger and won't get what he wants.

A positive approach:

A: I have been waiting for you to fix these windows for three weeks. Why hasn't the job been done in the time promised? I called several times and my calls haven't been returned. What happened?

B: Our secretary has left us and we haven't been able to find a replacement. We also had computer problems and urgently had to finish a big job before the weather changes. And I also had two men call in sick. I am really sorry for this and apologize. But I'll come next week and fix it, if that is okay with you.

A: The problem is that we have a big party this Saturday and it is really important that the windows be fixed by then. By the way, some of your clients will be at this party. Do you think that you can make an extra effort? I would really appreciate it.

B: I'll do my best and will try to delegate a man tomorrow. Thank you for your patience.

In this example, A didn't let his anger override his intention and remained responsive and sociable. To get what he wanted, he told the contractor that some of his clients would come to the party. The windows were fixed on time. This version of the conversation put no strain on the relationship and yet has motivated B to deal with the matter differently in the future.

Backing off

Sometimes opposing points of view are so inflexible that compromise is out of the question. If both parties stick to their opinions, not budging an inch and barely speaking to each other, it will be difficult to get back to rational debate and objectivity. At this point you must admit that, for the moment, you have no chance of getting what you want. But this retreat may just be temporary, indicating that the time is not yet ripe. How to soften the situation over a period of time is explained in Chapter 13, No Means Maybe.

Summing up

In this chapter you have learned that skill in getting what you want will get you only so far. If the atmosphere isn't favorable, you'll find it tough going. You should concentrate on cultivating a favorable atmosphere, establishing good relations with your partner, and overcoming divisive factors.

Step One

Get the Right Information

Chapter 4

Be prepared

Without a doubt, the key step in getting your own way is getting the right information. With good information, you have a better chance of reaching your goals.

The better the preparation, the better the prospects

When we're talking about getting the right information, we're talking about how to collect it, evaluate it, and make proper use of it. When you are better prepared, you are in a stronger position. A grasp of the essential information involved in a negotiation or strategy is essential.

In the negotiation of a deal or agreement, for example, properly prepared and presented information will give you a commanding position. The person with better information determines the course and duration of the negotiations, can weaken the other's argument, and is better prepared to come out on top. That is true in all areas of life, be it at the office, at the stock exchange, in the army, while visiting foreign lands, or even at home.

It is of the utmost importance that you invest sufficient time and energy in collecting, double-checking, and updating your information. It isn't always easy, but there are countless ways to discover all you need to know. It will be hard work, but the hard work will pay off in easier negotiations.

> *A sprinter practices every day, all year round, doing incredible amounts of work and preparation. But when the big race comes, the 100-metre dash lasts less than 10 seconds! Is it worth it? Of course it is. The more the sprinter practices, the better his chances of winning.*

This is no different from the work involved in getting what you want. Analyze cases where someone totally or partially failed in an attempt to get what they wanted, and you will make a startling discovery: almost every case ending in failure was the result of faulty preparation. The winners in these cases laid a better foundation through information.

Become a "spy"

To get the right information, you need to get into spy mode. Information is not likely to be handed to you on a silver platter. You must actively seek it out and just as actively process it. You will need to develop three solid techniques: asking questions, reading body language, and – most important – listening. Often you must attempt to piece disjointed fragments together. This can be dangerous because if you put the puzzle together incorrectly, your conclusions will be wrong.

> *A father got onto a subway train in New York City with two small boys. The pair were very noisy, banging into people and tearing newspapers out of passengers' hands. The father, a well-dressed businessman, sat in his seat with a sad face, his eyes closed. The mood in the overcrowded car became increasingly hostile toward the children. Finally the passenger seated beside the father nudged him roughly and demanded he take control of his children. The father opened his eyes, looked around*

*him as if he didn't know where he was, and then said
softly, but so that everyone could hear him, "I'm sorry,
we have just come from the hospital. My boys have just
found out their mother has died. Maybe that's why
they're acting up."*

You can see how important it is to collect information
before reacting. One or two short questions to the father, a look
at his face before giving vent to an angry rebuke, might have
defused the situation.

*A friend of mine vacationed in a five-star hotel in the
Caribbean and complained about the unclean room, the
noise, and other things. As no improvements were made,
he decided to leave the next day. The international chain
this hotel was part of had a cancellation policy of 48
hours, and my friend agreed to pay for this time. The
front office, however, insisted on payment for a week
because five days was "company policy for this hotel."*

*My friend held firm to his position. He would not pay
what they wanted. He logged onto the Internet and
searched for the name of the CEO of the hotel chain.
Then he went back to the hotel manager and told him,
without any aggressiveness in his voice, "I think that
your front office has made a mistake trying to charge
me for an additional five days. I am a good customer of
your hotels and know about your cancellation policy. If
you insist on charging the five days, I'll personally make
sure that Mr. X (and here he used the CEO's name) will
learn about the situation as soon as I am back."*

The result? He only had to pay for the two days.

My friend didn't know the CEO personally and didn't pretend that he did, but he would have written a personal letter to him. If the manager had asked him whether he knew the CEO personally, he would have left the question unanswered. As he was never asked, there was no need to go into details.

There are many situations in which some homework will benefit you. If you are meeting someone for the first time, for an interview or just a conversation, find out a little something about him or her beforehand. If you are dealing with a new line of business, you'll need information about the commercial practices in the new economic sector. When you apply for a job, research as much as possible about the company. If your firm is in a competitive field, you need information about the business practices, intentions, and plans of your competitors.

Chapter 5

How to gather information

We live in the information age. We have access to so many sources of information that it is almost overwhelming – the World Wide Web, libraries and research centers with electronic databases, businesses doing everything online, telephone books, business publications, extracts from commercial registers, tax statements and annual reports, to name just a few!

This is a real change from not so long ago when the gathering of information was for the few privileged, influential people who were in a position to collect and thus achieve power and glory. Consider the machinations of the Rothschilds surrounding the outcome of the battle of Waterloo in 1815. They had their agents strenuously gathering information on both the French and English sides of the battle. Armed with this information, Nathan Rothschild took up his position at the London Stock Exchange and began dumping hundreds of thousands of dollars' worth of government bonds. The word got around the floor that Rothschild knew that Wellington had lost at Waterloo. Soon everyone was dumping the government bonds (they were called consuls at that time) for the safety of gold and silver. It only remained for Rothschild agents, on a cue from their boss, to buy every government bond in sight for a song. Once the news of England's victory hit, the government bonds skyrocketed. When Napoleon met his Waterloo, the Rothschilds met their fortune!

Today information is available to everyone, but research can be a tiresome chore and therefore is easily neglected. This is a big mistake: you can form an initial picture of the origins, family relationships, status, and financial circumstances of a person or company just by checking out the resources I have mentioned.

Observing

You can acquire a great deal of information by observing people closely. The greatest care is needed here as it is foolish to judge someone only on appearances: clothes, car, etc. False trails are often deliberately laid. (More on this in Chapter 12, The Power of Body Language.) You can also learn by observing people in action or by watching closely as transactions take place.

> *A trader in an oriental bazaar asks a price of $100 for a Turkish coffee set. The tourist offers $10. The trader turns away indignantly and refuses to bargain. The tourist's counter-offer was so small that the trader took it as an insult. The invisible line of a taboo has been crossed.*

This example may not be world shaking, but every purchaser knows the dangers that may result when a counter-offer is poorly thought out: this alone can cause negotiations to become bumpy or even grind to a halt. Good information is vitally important for making a judgment on the crucial question of how far to go with a counter-offer. It would have been an easy matter for the tourist to find out by observation that she was expected to start at around $50, half the demanded price.

Relationship networks

The best and surest sources of information are available through networks of acquaintances, friends, and company insiders. The more people you know and the more attentively you listen, the better your network of relationships will be and the easier for you to obtain important information. One of the best ways to cultivate or enlarge your network is through informal events. While it may seem tedious to attend tiresome previews, monotonous birthday parties, unimaginative seasonal launches, and similar events several times a week, those who make this sacrifice (and I use the word deliberately) know that these events are their best sources of information. Only by appearing at public events again and again does one get the chance to discover valuable material.

Espionage methods

Just a quick comment on systems such as hidden microphones, phone-tapping, bugs, and so on. I vehemently reject these methods as they are unfair and also illegal in most countries. I believe that too much weight is given to information gathered in this fashion. There are other ways.

For a few years I was responsible for a discount-grocery chain. We were known for our aggressive advertising campaigns. They were so successful, they invited the envy of our competitors. One day we were surprised by four local police officers who came to search our premises. They interrogated employees, searched filing cabinets, inspected documents, and confiscated files.

It soon became evident that our strongest competitor was behind this. Because we always advertised the same product at a lower price in the same newspaper on the same day that his advertisement appeared, he suspected industrial espionage. The matter quickly petered out when the police found nothing. I never pursued it with the newspapers because I didn't want my secret to get out.

My secret? We kept our competitor's warehouse under regular surveillance. Whenever big trucks drove up with basic goods, cans of Coca-Cola, washing detergent, or toilet paper, we always knew that a campaign for these products was in the cards. No one would fill up a warehouse with such large quantities for no good reason. We knew our competitor must have been planning an advertising campaign for the next week, and presumably in the same newspaper and at the same price as last time, businesses being creatures of habit.

All we had to do was to offer the same item at a small percentage discount, and indeed this continued to work for years afterward. But please keep my secret to yourself!

How to screen information

We are bombarded with so much information nowadays that we are in danger of losing perspective. We no longer can differentiate between what is or is not significant. Radio, television, newspapers, and magazines all subject us to a constant stream of reports that for our own protection we quickly ignore, absorb or partially absorb, and judge as credible according to our own experiences. This is called automatic selectivity.

We should alternate between sources of information. We should never be solely dependent on just one informant, whether it be state-supported radio and television corporations, powerful publishing concerns, or big public-relations agencies with their sophisticated systems of information processing. There are information services everywhere: personal sources, the Internet, local radio programs, electronic data-banks, or information services with different political objectives.

By keeping your radar up, you can maintain a critical attitude toward all information. Common sense dictates that you should regularly check the reliability of incoming information and double-check it if any doubts about its accuracy emerge. Your experience and intuition will help you to screen for reliability.

You should automatically question each piece of information and consider whether the informant has some personal motive in sharing it with you.

The waiter in the restaurant suggests salmon. It's true that this item isn't on the menu, but he happens to have three portions left and highly recommends it. Should you begin to suspect that the chef wants to get rid of these portions because otherwise they will have to be disposed of? Of course you can still order the fish, and it might even be delicious, but you should be aware of the self-interest of the informant, in this case the waiter.

Another example:

You have given the order and now it's time for the wine. If you ask the waiter to recommend something, which wine do you think he will offer? If he has a head for business, naturally it will be the second most expensive (suggesting the most expensive would be too obvious). Or perhaps he is indeed a wine connoisseur and will give a carefully considered recommendation. Be that as it may, at least the idea of his having a personal interest in the matter should occur to you.

And one more:

James, a good friend of mine, tried to make money through commodity futures trading, a dangerously speculative practice. He had attended many seminars, read countless books, and daily sought expert advice. Despite this, he experienced constant losses. His failure was all the more surprising because he had all the necessary ingredients for success: he understood the broader economic picture, planned for the long term, and was prepared to take risks and accept losses. However, his streak of bad luck suddenly turned when he told his woes to an experienced financier, who gave him a deceptively simple but very effective piece of advice. What did the financier tell him? "Don't put your trust in experts! Be suspicious of advice given by a specialist, no matter how well known. Always test your sources of information against the little word 'Why.' You will be surprised…"

My friend followed his advice. When someone told him, "GE is a terrific buy today!" he immediately put this opinion to the test by asking, "What are you basing that on?" If the answer was a platitude, such as, "It's been too low for too long, it has to rise," my acquaintance would be very skeptical. However, if he got a reasonable answer, he realized he may have found a useful source of information. He became accustomed to framing his questions more loosely. Not "What is going to happen to the dollar?" but "Do you have an opinion on the dollar?" This way he gave the other person the option of not having to take up a position and saved a lot of time, filtering out idle chat and avoiding becoming burdened with useless information.

As time passed, my acquaintance refined his system and became very successful. He had learned to evaluate information. Today, specialists in the field ask for his opinion. The financier's advice literally was worth gold to him. (You will find more on this in Chapter 6, Practice a Little Skepticism.)

Putting what you've learned to good use

The most important quality for making practical use of the information you have gathered is creativity. Appropriately, then, rather than giving you a list of rules, I prefer to present three examples that speak for themselves.

Big ears

A company's board of directors found out just before their annual meeting that an opposing group of shareholders was planning to use the meeting to put forward a proposal that rumor had it would cause harm to the company. Through the grapevine, the company executives learned that the shareholders were well prepared and intended to congregate in a restaurant an hour before the meeting. The president of the board, a shrewd tactician, asked his secretary to take a seat at a nearby table and do nothing but keep his ears open. People in a group always talk loudly, so it was easy for the secretary to find out their strategy.

The result? In his opening speech, the president was able to refute the arguments of the opposition group and their proposal died on the boardroom table.

Tie a red ribbon...

The marketing director of a large firm needed to learn the turnover rate of a store up for lease. Because this store was still owned by one of the firm's competitors, a grocery chain, no reliable data were available. However, the total turnover rate was very important because the rental contract contained a turnover commission clause. The director approached this in two stages.

First, in order to ascertain the number of customers, he had an employee of the marketing department tie a small piece of red thread to five shopping carts and note the number of times they went through the tills in an hour.

Second, at the same time, he had "spies" note the totals on all the cash registers to establish the average sum spent by each customer.

With this readily available information, the director very easily calculated the turnover rate. The projection later proved very accurate. A little bit of brain-power and creativity go a long way...

In today's electronic age, this research would be substantially easier to obtain, by using discarded sales slips, as every slip shows a serial number, date, amount, and till number.

Sneaky

I observed the following scene in a crowded garden restaurant. A few people who were obviously unable to find any spare seats were standing around rather forlornly. One of them detached himself from the group and asked a waitress for the name of the headwaiter.

With charming smile and outstretched hand, he went up to the headwaiter, greeted him by name like an old friend, and inquired after his health. Of course the little group was at once shown to a table that had just become free. As I was leaving, I couldn't resist complimenting the shrewd man on his skill in getting what he wanted. The man admitted that the headwaiter was a complete stranger and that he had assumed the fellow would be unable to recognize all the people who called him by name.

Summing up

In this chapter, you have seen how information is gathered, examined, and applied. You also have had an opportunity to read a number of very different examples of using information in practical situations. Now it's time to start gathering and using information yourself.

Step Two

Investigate Motives

Chapter 6

Practice a little skepticism

Investigating the motives behind people's actions takes time and effort, but the benefits will far outweigh the work involved. People's up-front motives are not necessarily their real ones, particularly when the motives seem altruistic.

I believe a little secret skepticism is always in order. If it turns out that your skepticism was unfounded, there's no harm done and an error is soon corrected. This precaution keeps you grounded and protects you from disappointment. But be warned: by being on the look-out for real motives, you run the risk of losing certain illusions and becoming disenchanted with your relationships.

Why do you have to concern yourself with the real motives of the people you deal with? Because once you have identified them, you will get what you want. Everything you read in this book about conversation, listening skills, questions, answers, and observations serves only one purpose: identifying the true motive of the other party. If you succeed in that, you will truly possess the key to getting what you want.

The following illustrates how to apply these tactics successfully.

I was watching television with a visiting banker friend. The program revealed a group of Swiss companies' monopoly on cement. Every bag of cement bought in Switzerland passed through the hands of this group, which took its cut of the profit. The owner: "When we started up in this business, we found out that the people living in the mountains were forced to pay more for a bag of cement than the customers in towns or valleys. We thought this was wrong and saw to it that this discrimination ceased and everybody could buy at the same price."

He went on and on in this vein. This was said so earnestly that only a few viewers would have questioned his sincerely. However, my banker friend's dry comment, "And he laughed all the way to the bank," neatly summed up the truth of the situation.

Another example:

I'm sitting in a pub. At the next table are two well-dressed middle-aged gentlemen, businessmen or tourists. They are not alone for long. Two women soon join them, and I cannot help overhearing their conversation. According to the women, these men are splendid, remarkable, interesting, and entertaining. When one of the women makes a shamelessly exaggerated compliment about their good looks, I shake my head and wonder how many more compliments the men will be able to stand. Infinitely more, as it turns out, and the more champagne they order, the more freely the flattery flows. These women have, so to speak, found the key to their wallets.

Perhaps these men were naive, or maybe they only wanted to lose themselves in a fantasy, but if they had once stopped to think how the women would talk about them afterwards, they would certainly have had a rude awakening.

I realize that illusion plays a major role in our daily life, just as does the suppression of unpleasant thoughts and memories. However, this is not a book on psychology. These examples only go to show that what initially seem to be overly unselfish interests should be distrusted.

We always assume that others are rational beings. That's a dangerous assumption. Individuals are driven by emotions, desires, fears, and many other feelings and do not always apply reason. World history has been shaped again and again by irrational decisions, decisions that in many cases have led to war and to the annihilation of entire races and cultures.

It is just as wrong to believe that people always react rationally. Just take a quick look back at some hasty words you have said in anger and later regretted.

But how do we recognize what is genuine and what is false?

Nature has equipped us with an invaluable aid: gut feeling, or common sense. This, along with a healthy dose of skepticism, will help you immeasurably.

Using common sense, which we all know is not so common, should help us see the real reasons behind actions. If you are not so sure that this is true, think back to the previous example. What I'm getting at may not be pleasant, but it helps us see behind the mask.

Another example:

A group of heirs wanted to sell an industrial building. The property was situated on a first-class site in the center of a big city – a unique opportunity with regards to location and price. Offers came fast and thick. One of those interested told me later how he managed to exploit the real interests of the selling group, as well as those of their agent. Through skillful questions, this man found out that the agent, a chronically overworked lawyer, wanted to wrap the whole thing up as fast as possible. The aged heirs, on the other hand, were worried about the property falling prey to speculators and particularly wanted to avoid negative press reports.

Thanks to all this information, which, of course, he kept to himself, my acquaintance announced his firm intention of acquiring the property as a long-term investment and gave them a written declaration that for a whole year he would not raise rents or give anyone notice. He further offered to pay the legal costs of the transaction, as long as the matter was settled within two weeks.

Naturally, he obtained the property at a reasonable price, and it went on to prove itself to be a very sound investment, indeed.

Each of the other potential buyers could have come by the same information, and I am sure that some of them did. But it was only my acquaintance who had the idea of posing specific questions to discover the agenda of the other side.

The rules of the game

My friend's property purchase naturally involved a commission. The subject of commissions is worth some discussion. Let's say you want to buy a property or a business. Sooner or later the question of the agent's commission comes up, and often there is a statement to this effect: "The commission will be paid by the seller, which is to your advantage." However, it actually ties your agent's self-interest in with the seller's: the higher the price, the higher the commission. The seller and the agent, therefore, have a common interest opposed to your own. To alter this position, you should suggest that you will pay the commission, as long as the buying price is reduced by the amount of the commission. That is fair, and no one should refuse your proposal. You are now in a good position in the transaction, with the agent on your side, as he should be.

So what does all this mean? By solving the agent's concern about payment, by announcing your intention and stating the rules of the game, you have brought him over to your side. In effect, you have changed his primary interest. If you want to change someone's focus of interest, you must come up with a new inducement that is stronger and more promising than the old one. You must come up with arguments geared to and acceptable to him.

In most cases, we cannot change people's principal areas of interest. That would take more powerful forces than we can muster.

If it works for the advertising industry...

Discovering the other person's motives is the most important thing. But how do you find out the rules of the game? Every day the advertising industry carries out very direct research into the interests and needs of members of the public and applies this knowledge to marketing. We can do this, too, on a much subtler and more personal scale, with individuals.

In the past, a dishwashing machine was a privilege of the well-to-do. When mass production came into force and prices fell, a major marketing campaign, aimed at putting a dishwasher into every household, was launched. The campaign message was, "If you buy yourself a dishwasher, you will have more time to enjoy life."

But success proved elusive. It was only after market research discovered what truly mattered to housewives and their spouses that they succeeded. They changed their message to "... you will have more time for your family." This enabled homeowners to make their purchase with a clear conscience.

Many companies strive to connect with consumers' interests and to discover what their motivations are. Whole industries revolve around status symbols, creating needs and then satisfying them. Just consider how much money you would pay to acquire extravagantly expensive articles simply because a clever pitch convinced you that they are status symbols. What do the various gold and platinum cards of the credit-card industry symbolize? Their purpose – outwardly – is to help those who use them display their wealth. Looked at objectively, they are only an unnecessary security risk for the user, just like extremely expensive travel bags that attract the special attention of thieves hanging around the airport. High-prestige cars are thought to confer the level of status that the driver usually lacks. For some people, prestige items have only one purpose: to make them stand out from the crowd, to attract interest, admiration, and even envy.

On a slightly smaller scale:

A customer in a shop is hesitating about buying a particular dress. It is clear that the price is too high for her. One of the following arguments might convince her, despite the high price. "You can wear this dress on many different occasions – it takes the place of two others. It's also very easy to care for..." Or "This particular dress is custom-made. You're never going to run into someone else wearing your same dress."

If the customer buys the dress, the sales representative has succeeded in overcoming a strong motivation (thrift) with an even stronger one (vanity).

Another example: Many people put off going to the dentist until they are in agony, that is, until the primary drive (fear of dental appointments) has been overridden by a stronger drive (the elimination of pain).

A patient arrives at the dentist in terrible pain; the tooth may have to come out. A simple extraction costs little and takes only a few minutes. A root canal and a crown might easily cost ten times as much and will drag out over several sessions. How is the dentist to persuade the patient that saving a tooth is worth the expense?

The duty of the dentist is clear. If the tooth can be saved, then, from a medical point of view, a root canal has to be recommended. He tries to superimpose a new motivation by explaining to the patient how important it is to have your own teeth. The dentist has many different arguments: the practical argument (with a gap you can no longer chew as well); the aesthetic argument (the gap is unsightly); or the material argument (in any case, you would later require a bridge, and that is even more expensive).

A bit of detective work

Even the most extensive checklist would not be enough to investigate thoroughly the motivations of the person you are dealing with. Your powers of creativity and imagination also must be brought into play. You should ask yourself the following questions again and again:

❑ **Is her stated motivation credible?**

- ❏ **Does it stand up to critical scrutiny?**

- ❏ **Does it ring true?**

- ❏ **Am I receiving subconscious signals that could hint at other interests?**

Pay attention to your gut feelings. Observe your partner: eyes, reactions, gestures, dress, jewelry, shoes. That way you can find out a great deal. The way someone reacts is very revealing. Take note of things that escape the attention of others and remember them at the right time. It is important to persist, to build on your own skills so that you become surer and surer of your own instincts and learn to trust the evidence in front of you.

Summing up

Not everything you hear is true. If you want to know if people really mean what they say, find out their motives by asking the why question. Or, to put it another way, seek out their hidden agenda and act accordingly. Tune in to the other people. Listen to what they say and how they say it.

Chapter 7

How credible are you?

The other side of investigating the motives of others is knowing your own motives. This can be boiled down into the question of your own credibility. This is rarely written about in the context of getting your own way. But if you were to ask me what is the most important quality for succeeding, I would answer without hesitation: your credibility. Your credibility is sacred; it must be protected *at all costs*. You must *always* keep your word, regardless of the circumstances. Credibility is like innocence: once gone, it is gone forever.

There is a trade, dying out today, that symbolizes for me what I mean by credibility: that of the cattle-dealer. I grew up on a farm where my father bought and sold cows and calves. I can still recall the endless haggling between buyer and seller, until at last a handshake would settle things. There was no contract, nothing in writing; the handshake sealed the deal. Each party could rely on the word of the other. It was unthinkable that one of the two would break his word – doing so might be his commercial ruin.

But credibility often can be tricky to discern.

One day a judge was having his lunch in the park,

pleased to get away from the court for half an hour or so. A few minutes into his lunch, he noticed a disheveled man seated on a bench a few yards down the path. This man kept putting a brown paper bag to his mouth and seemed to be drinking from something inside it.

As a young man on a bicycle passed by the judge, a youth sprang from the bushes, knocked the cyclist down, and took off with his bike.

The judge thought he knew the thief – that the man had appeared before him in court a few months earlier. He even thought he remembered his name: Billy Padgett.

Meanwhile, the victim was calling out, "Police, police," because he saw a patrol officer not far away. The officer wanted to hear all about the theft and the judge volunteered his information. It seemed Billy Padgett would not enjoy his freedom much longer.

The officer also interviewed the only other eyewitness, the man with the paper bag. "I saw Bob Farley knock the man off his bike and make off with it," he said. "Bob Farley lives in my building. I think that's his name."

The drunk's statement was ignored and Padgett was arrested.

But the story has a happy ending. The "drunk" was no drunk at all but someone who needed an inhaler and didn't want other people to know about it. The real thief, Bob Farley, was arrested later.

This story shows that credibility can be misleading. Practically everyone is going to go with a judge's story over that of a seeming drunk!

Another example:

The police caught a local politician for driving while intoxicated. After he was stopped, he smiled at the police officer and told him that he drank only one glass of wine with his dinner that evening, nothing else. He stuck to this statement stubbornly.

However, breathalyzer tests and a double-check at the police station told another story. He was heavily intoxicated.

Of course he was handing the media a sensational story, which they dwelled on at length. It was the beginning of the end of his career. He would have been better off by telling the truth, however ugly or embarrassing.

It is not only your own credibility that is important, however. You also must be sure of your partner's trustworthiness. One way to ascertain his credibility is through active, inquisitive listening. In Chapter 11, The Power of Listening, you will learn how much information can be obtained by this method.

Step Three

Ask the Right Questions/

Give the Right Answers

Chapter 8

The art of questioning

Two monks, both heavy smokers, were unable to stop smoking during prayers. To solve this dilemma they each wrote the Pope a letter to get his opinion on the subject. Three weeks later they got together again and found to their surprise that the Pope had given only one of them permission to smoke. On comparing their letters, they found the explanation. The first monk had asked, "May I smoke during prayers?" and the answer was, "No." The second monk, however, had framed his question differently: "May I pray while I am smoking?"

The very fact that questions are such a powerful aid to communication means you must use them sparingly. Nothing is more irritating than a flood of meaningless questions. Anyone who behaves like this either is incapable of proper communication or is avoiding real conversation. A good question will elicit a reply and a counter-question and thus open a discussion.

Building bridges

Questions can build a bridge between people and form a basis for dialogue. Suppose you meet a friend who is facing a personal crisis. In such situations most people talk frantically about everything under the sun with the exception of the one problem that preoccupies their friend. But this facade is difficult to keep up.

If you ask sympathetic questions and show a willingness to help, on the other hand, you will have a more meaningful conversation. Voyeuristic, sensation-seeking questions of course are out of place, but you can work wonders with a question like, "Do you want to talk about your problem? I'm a good listener."

It is important to leave your counterpart the choice of answering so she can decide whether to carry on the conversation. Dialogue is a two-way street where each may approach the other. It doesn't matter whether you are dealing with a why question posed by a child or the great examples of rhetoric put forward by Socrates. If you consider the putting of questions you will realize that no other mode of communication lets you express your interest so clearly. You want to know something, you want to test reactions, elicit opinions, criticize, praise, or provoke – communication in its purest form.

Getting what you want involves possessing the powers of persuasion, which are often best used through asking questions. Before we formulate our questions and learn how to ask them most effectively, we must become clear as to the nature of questions, why we are asking them, and what the right ones are in different circumstances.

Wielding influence

Every question you ask will lead and influence the conversation taking place. In many situations you will want to plan and decide not just what questions to ask, but how you will word them, even how you will inflect them. The question, viewed as a means of argument, a method of persuasion, a way of getting what you want, has many facets. It can be used elegantly, like a foil by a fencer, with no intention of causing hurt. Or it can be applied dangerously and brutally, with the definite intention to hurt. I recommend the foil.

You can try this technique with a little experiment. Consider the next time you meet one of those socialites who waffle on forever. She will greet you with the standard question, "How are you?" and you can bet it will make no difference how you answer. That is where the fun begins. Try answering using intonation, posture, and facial expression that convey the answer, "Okay," but actually say, "I have a dreadful migraine, thanks. And how are you?"

She will most likely fail to take in what you said and will start to talk about herself. By asking the question, "How are you?" she has shown interest in you, but by posture and intonation, she has indicated something quite different: total lack of interest and the desire to get on as quickly as possible with her favorite subject, herself.

Every day we meet with this kind of discrepancy between what is said and what is meant. At first it is difficult to recognize, but through practice you can learn to pick up on the subtleties. It is important to remember that the revealing part of the question is not what is said, but what is left unsaid.

Why ask questions?

Questions can be used to test the person we are talking to, to intervene in a discussion and direct its course – in a word, to influence. Moreover, if skillful "test questions" elicit evasive answers, the very evasion reveals more than the other person intends.

Some time ago I worked with a money manager. We

talked daily on the phone. He often suggested I buy stocks from this or that company. I always came up with the why question.

"Why do you think this stock will go up?" I would ask.

Most of the time his replies were vague. He answered with banalities like, "We believe this company has potential" or "The price is low right now."

My next question would be, "How did you come to the conclusion to buy this stock?"

He almost never could give me a plausible reason. This made me realize that his advice was solely in his own interest, to generate commissions, which was his livelihood. We remained friends and years later he told me that my why question often took him by surprise, because most of his clients accepted his advice without further questioning.

It can be dangerous to say yes too fast and not question the other party's motives.

How do you ask the right questions?

In order to ask the right questions, you have to tune in to the person you are talking to and see things from her point of view. You need to listen and take in the whole situation. When you are clear about your intention and goals then you can make an effective plan and put it into action.

Basically we can divide questions into two main groups:

❏ Self-contained or closed-ended questions

❏ Open-ended questions

Self-contained questions

A self-contained question, often referred to as a closed-ended question, is one that can be answered with a definitive yes or no. "Is there any more spinach?" is a short, unproblematic question that is self-contained. It demands no addenda and fulfills its function with no complications. The answer is clear and unequivocal: either there is spinach or there isn't.

Self-contained questions

Purpose:	to get information
Advantage:	speed
Disadvantage:	they obstruct the flow of the conversation
Danger:	they can lead to a loss of control
Some examples:	"Are you feeling better now?"
	"Will you remain within the budget?"
	"Are you responsible for that?"
	"Did you post the letter?"
	"Have all the department heads been invited to the meeting?"
	"Did you book my flight?"

There is, however, no absolute certainty that your question will be answered with a simple yes or no. Every question can be answered evasively. Avoid posing questions that can be answered with a yes or no, unless they concern trivial matters.

Someone who answers yes or no has made up his mind and it will take a lot of energy for you to budge him.

> *A few years ago I was the boss of a mid-sized company that filled a niche in the market and was so successful that it aroused takeover interest on the part of our competitors. One unscrupulous competitor spread a rumor that the firm was up for sale. I found it fascinating to watch all the different reactions. Some of our competitors phoned up to ask directly if the firm was selling out. Just imagine my rival, who until then had turned our smallest error to his own advantage and with whom I had been doing daily battle, asking me if the business was for sale. Such a question leaves room for nothing but a clear and uncompromising no. Any other answer would destroy my credibility.*

In this example, my competitor committed every possible mistake. No attempt was made to play down a difficult situation. And the people asking questions had not considered my interest and had opted for the wrong means of communication, the telephone. What is especially interesting is the fact that a rival tried to get the whole picture on a complicated issue through a single forthright question. Most problems are time-consuming and cannot be dealt with swiftly by using a self-contained question. The only sensible forum to discuss such an important issue would have been a personal one-on-one meeting.

Open-ended questions

These questions are framed in such a way that they cannot be answered with a yes, no, or maybe. An open-ended question always gives rise to discussion and further questions.

Open-ended questions

Purpose: to help keep the conversation flowing, show interest in the opposing position, and make use of the information at your disposal

Advantage: you don't give up control

Disadvantage: you are dependent on the other person's cooperation. If he or she is in a bad mood and gives monosyllabic answers, you have nothing to go on. This approach is more time-consuming than asking self-contained questions

Beware: don't embark on a cross-examination. Don't bombard your discussion partner with questions. That would be counter-productive

Some examples: "What is your discount policy?"

"How long do you still need to work out your budget?"

"Who took over responsibility?"

"How many counters were open at the post office?"

"Who's invited to this meeting?"

Break important questions into stages

Now that we know the difference between the two main types of questions, let's look at my rival's question about my company (see example above). A better approach for him would have been to carry on the conversation face to face or have it arranged through a third party. Even if he was determined to use the telephone, it would have made more sense to break down our conversation into several stages, which would have allowed him to retain the advantage of flexibility. If we were interrupted or I lost my patience or took offence, he could have taken the matter up again later. Here is how you question in stages.

Stage one: Improving the atmosphere. You can do this with such questions as, "It's true that we're competitors, but today I'd like to talk to you about a personal matter…" Or "Are you busy right now?" Or "Do you have a moment to answer a delicate question?"

Stage two: Emphasizing your own credibility. "Even if we are business rivals, I have no difficulty in separating my business life from my private life. In this case, I'm calling about a private matter." Or "I'm phoning you person to person because I don't want anyone else to find out about our conversation."

Stage three: Asking the vital question. For example, "I've heard a rumor that in certain circumstances you might be interested in taking on a partner…" Or "Peter Smith [a mutual acquaintance] told me you would like to have the chance to turn your attention to a different field…"

Stage four: Eliciting a response. For example, "… and so I thought it would be a chance for another meeting on a personal basis. Would that appeal to you?" Or "It would be great to get together. Would you be interested?"

Breaking down questioning into these four stages, each leading to the next, makes success all the more likely. With this technique you never let control slip out of your hands.

But remember: timing is just as important as the method.

There is a right time for every question, and
that time does not necessarily have to be now.

In order to compare self-contained and open-ended questions, take a look at the following scenario and the different conversations.

You enter an electrical shop to buy a TV. On the shop
door you see a sign: "Prices as marked." Despite this,
you intend to wrangle yourself a discount. You are the
only customer and are being served by a salesman. You
see a TV you like.

Self-contained question: "Do you give a discount?"

In this example, the ready reply is "No!" as the salesman points his finger at the sign. On top of that, the exchange has acquired a hostile tone you could do without if you want to reach your goal of getting a discount. Or perhaps the salesman is in a good mood and says, "I'm sorry, we don't give discounts." Then you still have a faint chance, but your position has become unstable, and you risk surrendering control. In any case, the conversation is running counter to your interests.

Suppose the salesperson answers, "No, all customers pay the same price. We never give preference to anyone." You have lost control as he is now the one asking the questions and the flow of conversation is blocked. You have come up against a professional and for the moment have no choice but to retreat.

Now let's try this scene using open-ended questions. Note that the questions should not be asked aggressively. It is important to measure out the open-ended questions in appropriate doses. Beginners often fall into the error of asking questions far too rapidly, in the manner of an interrogator. This method leads to hostile feelings in the opposite party and an ultimate refusal to take part in the game. Here are some examples of what you should not do:

Q: "What is your discount policy?"

A: "We don't have one."

Q: "But I know you sometimes give discounts. Isn't that true?"

A: (hesitantly) "Yes, we have on occasion, but we don't usually, only in special cases."

Q: "So what's the story then? How much discount are you offering?"

A: (adamantly) "In your case, nothing. You see that sign over there? There you have it in black and white!"

In this conversation, the rules governing open-ended questions were followed, but all the opportunities were thrown away because of an aggressive approach. The same scene could have been played along the following lines:

Q: "What is your discount policy?'

A: "We don't really have any discount policy. We sell at the marked priced to everyone."

Q: "That's understandable. But I'm a regular customer. I've bought here on previous occasions. By the way, could you tell me about the..." (ask about some technical detail so as to change the subject and to avoid triggering the negative answer that hovers in the air).

Q: (after the technical question is answered) "Thanks for the advice. Now about the TV, can we reach an agreement on the discount for regular customers? What do you say to 10 percent?"

A. (counter-question by the salesman) "What was it you bought from us before?"

Q: "A radio from Mr. Jones. Does he still work here?"

A. "Oh, yes. All right, then, we'll agree to 10 percent."

The difference between these two examples is to be found in the all-important second question, which set the course. You still might lose in the end, in which case consider this to have been a practice run.

Open-ended questions lead automatically to a chain of single questions that all link up to a common purpose. In order to maintain the flow of questions, you should note the following rule:

*The subject for the next question
often lies in the previous answer.*

You should ask purpose-directed questions only if you have the relevant information. In our example you needed information about the policy of the business, the authority of the sales assistant, his mood, and product knowledge. We can use questions to obtain this kind of information.

Beside the main categories of open-ended and self-contained questions, there are other types of questions that are directed toward a specific goal. All these questions can be framed in an open as well as a closed style. They are:

- ❏ investigative questions
- ❏ deflecting questions
- ❏ association questions
- ❏ conversational questions

Investigative questions

Purpose: to acquire information and ideas, to help you decide how to proceed

Advantage: to elicit genuine, unadulterated information that would be difficult to obtain otherwise

Disadvantage: relatively time consuming

Beware: If your curiosity is too obvious, the person you are talking to will clam up

Examples: "I want to buy a computer. Which brand do you sell most of?" (This way you can assess the salesperson's competence and whether she understands her stuff.)

                     "I bought a computer from you two years ago. Is the warranty still valid?" (From this you can learn a little about the company's organization.)

                     "Who has taken over responsibility for that?" (This kind of question produces important information, if you have your eyes and ears open.)

A good investigative question should elicit data without the subject's being aware of the fact. You can achieve this by separating your questions into several parts. Most often you will begin with an open-ended question, as this leads to supplementary questions. The conversation can, however, veer in another direction and needs to be carefully brought back to your topic with deflecting questions (see page 108).

Another type of investigative question is the surprise question, or more accurately, the ambush question. This technique will not appeal to everyone. You end up pulling the wool over your opponent's eyes and making him betray something that he would really prefer to keep to himself. There are people who work this way, but I shouldn't have to point out to you that such questioning is unfair.

Experience shows that surprise questions are often counterproductive. They awaken aggression, create distrust, and warn of unfair attacks to come. Such questions come out of the blue and are said in the same tone as the rest of the conversation. The questioner doesn't change his or her expression, and the question is disguised as an innocuous afterthought. Some examples of surprise questions:

"Are you still beating your dog?"

"How much did you get for the sale of the house?"

"So how much do you earn a month?"

"Are you still dating Rosemary?"

Anyone who employs such questions counts on getting his "answer" in the non-verbal response, even if the question is not directly answered. This leaves you open to the danger of conjecture, not to mention that if the other person discovers what you are up to, you will appear in a poor light.

Deflecting questions

Deflecting questions are specific questions posed with the intention of changing the direction of conversation.

Deflecting questions

Purpose: redirecting the conversation

Advantage: they prepare the way for a change of topic and point the conversation in the desired direction

Beware: deflecting questions must be handled very subtly or your intention may become immediately apparent. On the other hand, if your change of topic is not precise enough, the discussion may slip out of your control. If the change of direction occurs abruptly, the other person will become suspicious or annoyed, which is counterproductive to your goal.

In the earlier example, looking for a discount at an electronics store, if the salesman had replied to our request for a discount with the statement, "No, I'm sorry it's not possible," a conceivable, albeit very direct, deflecting response might be (with a smile): "What do I have to do to make it possible?" However, it is usually better to avoid direct questions altogether.

An example:

You are at a party and the host is regaling the guests non-stop with tales of his safari in Kenya. The entire group is bored stiff. You would like to change the subject, but he hardly lets anyone get a word in edgewise. He relates every detail of the trip and currently is talking about the little plane his group flew on their safari. The conversation might go something like this:

Host: "... and the wind was like a hurricane. We were tossed around in this tiny little plane and..."

You: (without hesitation) "Were you wearing seat belts? Did the plane even have any?"

Host: "Actually, the plane did have belts, thank God, and of course we wore them, even though the crew didn't bother to check."

You: "I've always wanted to know how long the flight to Kenya is. It must be an extremely long trip. What time did you take off?"

And from here you can divert the conversation to duty-free shops, Kenyan food, and similar subjects. In any case, you are off the topic of the safari. You have taken control of the conversation

Another example:

Let's assume you want to return something to a store but have lost the receipt. How would you approach the store manager? As I often have done myself, you probably would try to tell him when you bought the item, that you lost the receipt, that you are sorry but you are a good customer, and so on. But this makes it easy for him to say, "Sorry, company policy." Once this is said, you will have a hard time persuading him.

I learned an interesting twist on situations like this from Ron, a friend of mine. He regularly uses the phrase, "I need your help..." This small sentence changes the whole approach right at the beginning. You don't have to be defensive. You can reduce your explanation to a minimum. The appeal to the other person's helpfulness works most of the time. But there is one important thing to keep in mind. It only works if you don't forget to put on a nice smile while saying the magical words!

Deflecting questions are also important in the closing stages of a conversation. Let's assume the other person is reluctant to wind it up. He goes on and on, but even though you've got another appointment, you don't want to offend him by cutting him off. What do you do? What shouldn't you do? Don't keep glancing at your watch or holding it up to your ear to see if it's still ticking. Don't bundle your papers and pack them away and insert, "Well..." into the conversation. Instead, use association questions.

Association questions

A subtler method to use, already in everyone's possession, is the power of association. Association is defined in the dictionary as "something linked in memory, thought or imagination with a thing or a person; the formation of mental connections between sensations, ideas, memories, etc." Using this technique you can turn the conversation any way you want.

For example, find out ahead of time what the other person is planning to do after your meeting and you will be able to bring this topic into your conversation at the right moment. Let's assume you find out at the start of the conversation that she has an appointment with her investment adviser immediately after. Mention something associated with this. Tell her about your own experience in money matters or ask if she can recommend an investment adviser. This will remind her of her appointment and she can start to wind up the talk with your guiding hand. If you don't have specific information about her next appointment, mention driving home, construction, the chaotic traffic, etc.

Using association to influence the other person does not always work, especially if there are several people taking part in the conversation. Sometimes you have to make two or three attempts to attain the desired result.

Another tactic: Near the end of the conversation, switch to the past tense and that will draw the talk to a close.

An example:

I received the address of a new medical practitioner from a friend and made an appointment for a first meeting. After about 15 minutes of discussion and history taking and just before I wanted to give him some additional information about my medical history, he suddenly leaned across the table, extended his hand and said: "Have a good day." He had signaled that the conversation was over.

It would have been so easy for him to choose another, less insulting way, but he hadn't read this book! Speaking in the past tense, he might have said, "Was there something else that you wanted to share with me?" or "It was nice to have met you," and I would have known that he wished to terminate the meeting.

Using deflecting or association questions is a personal choice. Test both methods and use whichever style suits your personality, while remaining as charming as possible and avoiding obvious breaks in the conversation. If you want to terminate the conversation, use the past tense.

Leading questions

Purpose:	to directly influence someone
Advantage:	can be a quick way to get the desired response
Disadvantage:	these questions work only with beginners; they annoy experts. I recommend only limited use
Examples:	"You like this picture, too, don't you?"
	"Am I right in thinking…"
	"Surely you don't want to go out again either when it's so late…"
	"I don't suppose you mind if…"
	"You don't like Californian Wine, do you?"
	"But you agree with me that…"

The skill of asking leading questions is commonly extolled as the great art of interrogation and is practiced and refined in training courses. I do not share this opinion. No matter how subtly leading questions are phrased, they are usually recognized for what they are and leave the other person with a feeling of being at your mercy or of not being treated as an equal. The unconscious mind registers the pressure inherent in this form of questioning and reacts with aggression, resignation, or lack of interest. These are all unnecessary handicaps, which we want to avoid. Leading questions are nearly always clumsy, and those who use them regularly should not be surprised if their advances are met with resistance.

Conversational questions

Questions that do not fall into the above categories belong to a large group, conversational questions.

Conversational questions

Purpose:	to fill gaps in the conversation, to encourage the other person, and to set the mood
Advantage:	they demonstrate interest, smooth over tricky situations, provide space for thought, and help camouflage direct questions
Disadvantage:	a tendency to deteriorate into small talk
Examples:	"Why do you recommend this model?"
	"What else is new?"
	"How are you?"
	"Have you heard..."
	"How was your holiday?"

Most questions asked during conversation consist of harmless chatter, which is precisely why they are so useful. They readily lend themselves as a cover, preparing the way for the all-important information questions and deflecting questions you need to ask to get your own way.

Questions yield information

You can discover your partner's likes, disposition, lifestyle, and hobbies and use this information to establish an atmosphere favorable to getting your own way. But you must have a genuine interest in the person you are talking to. As a rule, this is the main factor in deciding the success of a conversation or an entire business deal.

Supplementary questions

You will come across people who are masters at giving evasive answers. For example, they choose to use warmth, conciliatory phrases, and lots of charm.

> *I heard an interview on television once in which a journalist asked a US General when they were going to attack Iraq. This was an unanswerable question in the tense situation that the world was in at that time. He could have responded that he couldn't answer this question. By doing so, however, he would have been rude to the journalist. He chose a more elegant solution and said, "I'll try to answer your question with a reference to the Vietnam War..." He went on to talk about that war, without even mentioning Iraq. He clearly did not answer the question. I would bet that most people didn't even realize it.*

Of course you won't fall into that trap, because you will keep up the "interrogation" and repeat your question later and in different words.

We conclude this chapter on questions with the story of a manufacturer who through skillful questions managed to save a company. I leave it to him to tell the tale:

I am Paul Alexander (not his real name) and I manage a medium-sized manufacturing firm producing men's shirts for retailers. During the recession a number of years ago, my customers began to go for cheaper goods from Hong Kong and Italy. My turnover fell sharply. I wanted to hold on to all my staff as long as possible, but the problems were pressing and I sought new ways to recover the lost turnover.

One day I came into chance contact with a business specializing in telephone sales. The idea was to sell directly to the individual. The company was very successful and the method impressed me. Could this system be imported to Europe?

My American friends explained that interest had to be stimulated with the very first sentence of the phone call, with the perfect phrasing of that question. It is possible to ask the same thing in countless different ways, but only one way of wording is just right and it was important to identify this.

Back in Switzerland I began to experiment and I soon worked out the right way to frame the question: "My name is Alexander from Alexander Shirts. We make shirts for men. I have just one short question."

Now came the critical moment: "If you could buy your shirts directly from the factory, made to measure, at a price of $30, would you be at all interested?"

This question saved our firm. It gave us the possibility of marketing directly to high-end customers and brought us desperately needed orders. The rest was word of mouth and today we employ more people than ever and the new sales department has become a flourishing part of our business.

Summing up

We have discussed many aspects of questions including the difference between open-ended and self-contained questions. You have also learned which wording to use, how to control the conversation through questions, and how to obtain information.

Important as questions are, they are only one side of the coin, since every question requires an answer We now know that there are quality questions and there are also quality answers. The latter are the subject of the next chapter.

Chapter 9

The art of answering

Everything you say must be true,
but not everything that is true must be said

Asking questions is the black belt of the art of persuasion. To be able to fully practice this art, you also must be able to give the right answers, so that a skillful question can be at least partly neutralized. Answering is not just a case of slipping into a passive role and responding to questions; every answer contains the chance to influence or take control of the conversation.

To be on the safe side, assume that the person asking the questions is just as cunning an expert as you and that she is well up on the dynamics of controlling a discussion. If that turns out not to be the case, all the better for you.

It is difficult to put up a defense against unfair questions and it is even harder, in such a situation, to keep your cool and not let yourself be provoked. I advise against getting into such conversations in the first place. If you do find yourself in the middle of one, however, you must be able to withstand "the pain of provocation," while always remaining pleasant and cordial.

Even so, sometimes you just can't resist closing an unfair discussion with a quick-witted answer that might be considered provocative by the interviewer. This is especially so when you are interviewed in front of the public, be it on radio or TV. Here is an example that I found on the Internet, in which someone attached, as the best example of a comeback line he had ever heard, an exact transcript of a National Public Radio (NPR) interview between a female broadcaster, and a US Army General who was about to host a Boy Scout Troop at his military installation.

Interviewer: So, General, what things are you going to teach these young boys when they visit your base?"

General: We're going to teach them climbing, canoeing, archery, and shooting."

Interviewer: "Shooting! That's a bit irresponsible, isn't it?"

General: "I don't see why. They'll be properly supervised on the rifle range."

Interviewer: "Don't you admit that this is a terribly dangerous activity to be teaching children?"

General: "I don't see how. We will be teaching them proper rifle discipline before they even touch a firearm."

Interviewer: "But you're equipping them to become violent killers."

General: (presumably looking at her from top to bottom) "Well, you're equipped to be an exotic dancer, but you're not one, are you?"

(The radio went silent and the interview ended.)

This is an exception, of course. As a rule, playing fair is the best way to get what we want. So we should do all that we can to avoid unfair situations and to resist getting taken in by them. However, if in spite of all this you do one day find yourself pressed into the role of victim, you should at least learn how to defend yourself against unfair methods.

Never, ever let yourself be provoked!

I know a radio station that broadcasts a weekly chat show. To make it more entertaining, the host acts in a highly unorthodox manner. He asks the invited guests unfair questions, attributes to them remarks that were never made, draws absurd inferences, and insults them freely. It is painful to witness how helpless most quests, among them experienced managers, entrepreneurs, and public figures, behave in the face of his unfair interrogations. Many have no idea how to defend themselves.

Provocation is the most dangerous trap anyone can set for you. Be on your guard and don't fall in!

We are all susceptible to certain words or associations that can cause us to snap and react in an uncontrolled way. An unfair sparring partner will try to identify and then push these buttons. It takes strength of nerve to stay cool and collected in such circumstances, particularly if you are naturally hot-blooded. All the same, you must control yourself and remain cordial no matter what happens. If you allow yourself to be provoked, you have already lost the battle. However, if you manage to keep your cool and stay fair and composed, you have a chance, even if your sparring partner is stronger, better informed, and more articulate.

The most treacherous conversation tactic is the personal attack. Instead of confronting your objective arguments, your opponent assails you on a personal level, in matters having to do with your lifestyle, your religion, your skin color, your way of life. If the attack concerns an earlier indiscretion that may be common knowledge, you can get out of it with a dash of humor. Otherwise, you must try to separate the personal attack from the matter at hand, to pass off the insult with an aside, or to ignore it and address only the issue under discussion.

> *"You surely don't expect me to answer that allegation; but to the case in point I want to say this..."*

Or something along the lines of:

> *"You're confusing the issue; we're supposed to be discussing..."*

A counter-question is also very effective:

> *"Could you please frame that question in a more positive way?"*

Or even better, take control of the situation yourself with the following:

> *(pause) "First of all, I'll try to frame your question in a slightly more positive way." Then you repeat the question, worded differently, and then conclude by answering it without hesitation.*

Another good answer to a malicious question is this sentence:

> *"My head wants to believe you, but my heart won't."*

Or:

"Will you forgive me for not answering? Then I'll forgive you for asking such a question."

If you are getting fed up, try to redirect the conversation with the help of the following sentence, spoken in a friendly tone:

"I have the feeling we're not conducting a dialogue, but just exchanging insults. Let's focus on the arguments I've presented. For example..."

Everyone finds it hard to suffer provocation without retaliating. As rage builds up inside you, your heart begins to race, adrenalin is released, and your breathing falters – how can you pretend to be not affected?

I know of only two ways to protect yourself from the danger of overreacting.

The first is breathing. Even as the first note of provocation is sounded, take deep breaths and practice belly-breathing. With a little practice, you can do this so discreetly that no one will notice. Steady breathing gives you a chance of answering in a calm voice.

The second protection is to discuss your emotion openly, but calmly:

"I see we have a serious misunderstanding, which we will have to clear up. For the moment, however, I want to concentrate on the matter at hand, and say this about it..."

In this way you divert attention, avoid stoking the flames, and gain time to prepare a considered response.

You can also try coping with an affront by pretending not to have heard it, dealing instead, quietly and calmly, with the real matter at hand. Expressing understanding for your partner's fury/irritation/bad temper/annoyance ("I understand you are upset but…") might work, but it allows you to be drawn into a fight. It is better to maintain long pauses and slow the pace of the dispute.

If all this proves useless and an argument seems inevitable, break off the conversation or you will descend to the same unfair level as your partner. If you wish to fight, attack can be the best means of defense, but only if you are well-versed in the art and well prepared.

Here are a few more tips that will enhance the efficiency of your responses to questions.

Creative thinking

Creative thinking is essential for giving effective responses. This is more easily said than done, as you have to think on the spot. If you memorize a few ground rules and practice them over and over, it will not be hard to improve your response technique. The very fact that you are preparing is a point in your favor. Very few people take the trouble to do this!

No half-truths

Your response must always be technically correct. Half-truths are dangerous because they can easily be turned against you.

Never give direct answers to awkward questions

Do not answer awkward questions directly, but rather by being a little vague. For example, "Do you imagine that…" or "If…, then…" Whenever possible, use the subjunctive (conditional mood) rather than the indicative (realistic mood). "I would…" not "I am…"

A friend of mine likes asking questions. He apparently doesn't realize that there is a fine line between personal interest and nosiness. Some of the questions could be considered offensive, for instance when he asked someone, "Are you going to marry that girl?" or "Will you have any more children?" It is interesting to see how people react to his questions. Some are offended and choose not to answer at all. Others answer truthfully, although with some embarrassment. I just laugh and tell him that he asks his questions for shock value. Then I thank him for the amusement he has given me. He very rarely questions me these days.

Pose counter-questions

It is possible to parry critical questions by asking counter-questions. However, this method is so well known that it rarely works. The other person might challenge with, "Why don't you want to answer my question?" And this would be one-up for the other side.

Call the question into question

When you have to rescue yourself from a critical question, this method is quite reliable. Politicians are masters at it. Examples:

"You're asking the wrong question, Mr. Smith…"

"First I would have to examine your figures to find out the basis for our different opinions."

Or you could try this:

"I question the accuracy of your figures, but I will nonetheless answer your question."

Then choose the particular part of the question that you want to answer.

Be wary of overly friendly questions

Always remain outwardly polite and cordial but inwardly alert and skeptical. A nice question often is used to lure you onto thin ice. If an interviewer famous for taking a tough line suddenly takes the soft approach, be on red alert. The same goes for casual conversations and business discussions.

Separate your answers into parts

Just as complex questions should be asked in stages, so difficult answers should be broken down into simple parts. At first answer only the part of the question you feel sure about, leaving the rest until later. In the majority of cases, you can safely assume that the issue will not be raised again. (Unless, of course the questioner has read this book!)

The importance of "how" matching "what"

Your non-verbal message (gestures, facial expression, tone of voice) must match the factual information you give out. Otherwise it comes across as grating, artificial, and scarcely convincing. This has a lot to do with your personal sincerity. It could well be that the other person does not consciously perceive any discrepancy, but she will sense it subconsciously and react irritably. Even worse, she will question your credibility.

In public, only the audience matters

When you are interviewed in public, don't treat the interviewer as a single individual but consider the members of the audience and address your responses to them. This applies even when your audience consists of an invisible mass of radio listeners.

The following examples are based mostly on my experiences in business and powerfully illustrate how you can dodge the dictates of the question and take control. It should not be difficult for you to find further examples in your own life. I suggest you experiment with the various scenarios here.

Q: "You hold a senior position in the business community. How did you come by it?"

A: "I was looking for a job and came across it by
(wrong)   chance."

A: "Do you recall that five years ago the Smith
(right)   Financial Firm made headlines?" (Pause) "Their circumstances really caught my attention."

Q: "Your prices are much lower than those of your rivals. Something a bit fishy there, surely?"

A: "Oh, but we are one hundred percent above
(wrong)   board. Otherwise do you think our customers…"

A: "Do you imagine we could stay in business so
(right)   long using underhanded methods?" (Pause) "Our rivals would come down on us like a ton of bricks…"

Q: "Your prices are much higher than those of your competitors. Are you being unfair to your customers?"

A: "What are you suggesting? Really, I can't
(wrong)   believe this. In any case…"

A: "Be careful not to compare apples and oranges.
(right)   We check our competitors' prices every day. But you couldn't say we're one of the cheapest either.

Our prices reflect not only the product but also the exceptional service and after-sale customer service. Customer satisfaction is extremely important to us."

Q: "How much do you earn, by the way?"

A: (wrong) "No comment. That is a private matter."

A: (right) "Why are you asking this?"

Q: "Why did you only stay six weeks at your last job?"

A: (wrong) "I didn't like the atmosphere at work…"

A: (right) "I quickly established that this position didn't meet my expectations, and I didn't want to waste any more time than absolutely necessary."

Here is a tip on how to conduct yourself at an interview for a new job. I learned it from a firm specializing in staff recruitment. As soon as possible, grab the chance to ask a question of your own. It goes without saying that you should do this in a relaxed, charming way, with a pleasant smile. For example, if you ask the following question you will find things noticeably easier afterwards:

"I want to be sure that I fully understand what the position (the job advertised) involves. Could you tell me briefly what you would expect of me?"

If you have learned to listen properly, you will pick up appropriate phrases that you can later insert, suitably reworded, into your own responses.

Summing up

Every question demands a reply. Only those who have mastered the technique of answering can stand up to a trained questioner. This chapter dealt with the various qualities of an answer. It is especially important to remember this: never, under any circumstances, allow yourself to be provoked. Double-check the examples on how to respond to unfair attacks.

Chapter 10

The art of speaking

This little joke shows the power of a few well-chosen words, spoken at the right time:

> For many years a small boy's parents, siblings, teachers, and psychologists had tried everything to get him to speak, but from the day he was born not a word had ever passed his lips. Nothing worked, neither words of encouragement nor words of punishment.
>
> One day, during lunch, the moment came for which they had all been waiting. Without warning, the boy looked reproachfully at his mother and said loudly and clearly, "This soup is too salty."
>
> In the midst of all the excitement that followed, his father asked why he had never previously spoken. "Until now, the food was always fine," mumbled the boy, and then he fell silent again.

No other subject has been so exhaustively discussed as the desire to influence others by means of the spoken word. The desire to learn effective speaking has created a whole market of books, cassettes, videos, and seminars offering considerable insight into the lofty art of rhetoric. Today, anyone can develop his skills to the level of a professional speaker. This is great news for getting your own way, as the manner in which you express yourself has enormous significance.

Speaking one-on-one

We often see the following:

> *One person speaks and the other listens. Or rather, she assumes the gestures, posture, and look of a listener. In actual fact, she is already preparing her own answer and only hears what she wants to hear. No sooner has the speaker paused for breath than she rushes in with the reply, which appears to follow what has been said, but immediately takes an entirely new, personal path. This game repeats itself throughout the so-called conversation, but there is no attempt at real dialogue. The pair are not talking to each other, but past each other.*

So what is the best way to make yourself understood and achieve your goals? By going one-on-one, person-to-person, in your dealings. This means finding out, taking into account, and accepting the degree of intelligence, the interests, and the temperament of the person you are talking to. Once you have established a genuine dialogue then you will achieve proper communication. Only words spoken on a person-to-person level are really taken in. Let's explore how to go about this and what you must look for in the process.

Put yourself in your partner's place

Relating on a partnership level does not mean totally integrating yourself with partner or adopting his style of speech or mannerisms. A quiet, refined person who suddenly uses strong language to keep up with someone is rightly seen as phony. Instead, make a real effort to understand and appreciate the other person's motives and argument, even if they are light years away from your own position. This is much more difficult than you might think as you must first empathize with the other person without surrendering your own position. However, it is precisely by investigating the opposite point of view that we often discover the original basis for our own point of view, which helps us put new force into our own arguments.

Style and content must agree

We are constantly sending out signals during our speech. While we are choosing our words, we are also sending out unconscious signals with our tone of voice, gestures, facial expressions, and body language. If the content of our message does not agree with these signs, trained listeners will begin to doubt the veracity of the words and they concentrate on obtaining proof of this lack of authenticity. Now your conversation is no longer on a partnership level, nor is the other person listening properly to what is said. Even an untrained listener subconsciously senses disharmony between content and non-verbal messages. They feel uneasy, without being able to pinpoint the exact reason why.

You can learn to control your body language and tone of voice. I strongly recommend training courses and reading material. You can even sign up for a few lessons with a singing teacher to develop vocal and breathing techniques. Learning these skills is well worth the effort.

Language is one of the most important and safest aids to assess another person. Only by continually observing what goes on during a conversation will you know if your message is getting through and how to adjust your tone of voice, your expression or your style of language. The purpose of a conversation is to have your information accessed by the other person. This occurs only once you reach the level of one-on-one partnership.

Never cause hurt

You govern your words,
but once uttered, they govern you.

–Scottish saying

No matter what your circumstances or what you have to say, your intonation and choice of words should never cause hurt. Keep aggression out of your voice. If it threatens to creep in, smooth your tone at once, especially in an aggressive situation. On the other hand, an extremely flat or seductive tone is also out of place. Take care to use your own natural, unaffected tone.

As for your actual words, say what you have to say clearly and simply. As you go further into the dialogue, with a good back-and-forth discussion of questions and answers, abstain from using harsh words. They inevitably lead to talking in circles and produce nothing but unnecessary hostility. Everything can be said in a variety of ways. "You are a liar!" sounds different from, "Are you sure you've not somewhat embellished the facts?" or "I've a feeling you're maybe misleading us a bit there."

Examples:

instead of "stingy" you could say "thrifty"

instead of "impertinent" perhaps "outspoken"

instead of "talkative" you could say "sociable"

instead of "a spendthrift" you could use
"living the high life"

In most circumstances, you will have no difficulty in finding a suitably neutral substitute for a harsh expression – unless you deliberately want to cause hurt, which, as I said earlier, doesn't pay because it always backfires.

I recently noticed a photographer taking detailed shots of the area around my house. I assumed she was an inquisitive reporter and was about to ask her, "What are you doing?" I stopped myself in time and asked instead, "What do you see with your professional eye?" As it turned out, she had no interest whatsoever in me, but was photographing street scenes. An interesting conversation developed that would have been scarcely possible if I had used my first choice of words. She was not forced to be on the defensive and neither was I.

Many people try to impress their companions by inserting foreign or obscure words into their conversation. The following little episode I overheard makes me smile to this day.

A group of women was discussing eating problems and how hard it was to resist everyday temptations. A very stout lady was obviously getting irritated by all the talk about her problem, and butted into the conversation to declare that she happened to suffer from hyperorexia, an unfortunate illness for which doctors had not yet found a remedy. The lady had achieved her goals. The group changed the subject. Later, when I looked up this exotic ailment in the dictionary, I had to laugh. "Hyperorexia" means nothing more or less than "eating disorder"!

Notwithstanding this humorous example, I recommend using big words sparingly; otherwise you run the risk of being seen as a show-off.

The ground rules

Now that the concept of speaking on a partnership level is understood, I want to highlight the six points I consider to be the most important in persuasive speaking.

1. Vary the rhythm of your speech

Alter your voice between quick/slow and loud/soft. Above all, avoid falling into an expressionless monotone. Changes of rhythm should not occur abruptly but should correspond smoothly to what is being said. Facts should be pronounced objectively, clearly, and in a steady voice. Speak your opinion with more flow, in modulated tones and with lots of pauses.

2. Speak naturally

Superb speaking skills might not lead to truly effective speaking. In fact, people can develop excellent skills – their arguments may be brilliantly formulated and their discourse interspersed with artful rhetoric, with some of those incomprehensible words for impact – but still fail to communicate. Their impressive performances are not the way real people speak; they are unable to achieve a true one-on-one discussion.

Brilliance is not what is required, but rather clarity. It is great if you can tune into your partner's wavelength and still manage to convey your message clearly and concisely. This is what I call a successful conversation.

3. Speak clearly

Speaking as precisely as possible carries conviction. Pronunciation is of critical significance. Pay special attention to the end syllables of your words as you don't want to lose your message in a mumbled mess. However, it is also important to be natural; it will sound phony if you enunciate the end syllables too strongly.

4. Stick to your subject

Present your subject with precision, in such a way that your listeners can follow it without difficulty and without losing the train of thought. Don't stray off your subject with asides and tangents or your listeners will tune out. It is tiresome to listen to someone express himself in a complicated way, prattling on and on with irritating asides and imprecise ideas. Why risk your listener switching off and letting their thoughts wander? You will miss your chance to get what you want.

When giving a speech, take particular care with new ideas that creep into your thoughts during delivery. Even if they seem to you to be brilliant flashes of inspiration, such notions can push you off topic and make you lose your train of thought. Stick to your script and cue cards.

5. Keep the content relevant

Empty phrases will not hold the attention of your audience. Meaningless twists of words will only confuse them and make them weary. (You may on very rare occasions actually wish to do this, but they are few and far between.) The old rule, "If you have nothing to say, say nothing," still holds true.

Your speech should be clear and relevant to your listeners. This means you must prepare and present the topic differently every time to suit the particular audience.

6. Be careful when using negative points

This is especially important in one-on-one conversations. Present negative points indirectly, by way of hints. Instead of saying, "I am very disappointed in you," try, "I felt disappointed when…" Even if the whole matter seems hopelessly negative, you will be astonished by how many positive aspects you can find if you look hard enough.

Before making a negative point, mention something positive. When you juxtapose the positive and the negative points, you should be sparing with the word "but." This word tends to cancel out all that was said before it.

Example: "I have always enjoyed working with you, *but* some information has come my way." The unsaid part reads, "so I didn't really enjoy working with you." This may not be true. It would be better to say, "I have always enjoyed working with you, and your team had achieved considerable success. If my information is correct, something has happened that we have to talk about."

Summing up

This chapter touched on only the most important points about persuasive speaking. It is a never-ending topic! I wanted to demonstrate to you what is essential and help you to adapt it to your individual style. Everyone can develop his or her own potential. You may want to consider enrolling in a public-speaking class. Remember, though, that courses and books are only a beginning. Practice, practice, and yet more practice, along with encouraging criticism from trusted friends and colleagues – these are key to success.

Step Four

Listen
Actively

Chapter 11

The power
of listening

Many marriages would still be intact,
if she or he had learned to listen.

We often witness the following scene: One person speaks and the other listens. Or rather, he assumes the gestures, posture, and look of a listener. In fact, he is already preparing his own answer and only hears what he wants to hear. No sooner has the speaker paused for breath than he rushes in with the reply, which appears to follow what has been said, but immediately takes the "conversation" down a whole new, personal path. This game repeats itself throughout the conversation, but there is no attempt at real dialogue. The pair are not talking to each other, but past each other. There is a huge difference between just hearing and really listening.

For many people the word "listen" means only that they are listening for the other party to pause for breath, so they can leap into their own side of the conversation. Check out the following dialogue.

> *Female:*   *"Last night I went to a performance of Mendelssohn's violin concerto in E-minor..."*
>
> *Male:*   *"What a coincidence! I heard some classical music yesterday, Beethoven's Ninth Symphony..."*

Female:	*"Mendelssohn is so romantic, I was quite entranced and..."*
Male:	*"The first three movements of the Ninth are not all that well known, but the fourth..."*
Female:	*(falteringly) "... and began thinking about my marriage and the future..."*
Male:	*"Yes, we must talk about it sometime. Beethoven is so magnificent..."*

Let us end this conversation before it sinks any lower. This pair could carry on until the cows came home and still get nowhere because the male character has never learned to listen. He should be told to shut up! His thoughtless chatter has spoiled the chances of a constructive conversation about their personal lives.

We are just like him most of the time. Instead of listening to what our conversation partner is saying and how he or she puts it, we only pretend to take in what is said. We don't bother really listening to the true content. Instead, we deceive the other party by our fake expression of interest and corresponding body language. While the other is still speaking and when we should be listening, we are preparing our own response. We eagerly await the slightest pause in the flow of words in order to bring in our own arguments. Once started we are even afraid to allow ourselves a pause for breath, in case the other will take advantage of it.

In my capacity as a business consultant, I regularly talk to managers in many different lines of work. I meet precious few who are good listeners. It seems that many business people are tireless windbags who suffer from the stress of constantly having to prove themselves and who richly deserve the label "talkaholic."

Recently, I met the CEO of a fairly large engineering firm in order to ask him some questions. From start to finish of our conversation he spoke continually without expressing a grain of curiosity as to why I was there. I found it impossible to get a question in edgewise. When, after half an hour, I sourly took my leave, his last remark was, "Sometimes I think I talk too much…" I made no comment. Any criticism would have fallen on deaf ears. I had no recollection of what he said in the course of his monologue – my attention wandered from the very beginning – and my questions were never even asked, let alone answered!

Successful listeners are always conscious of the danger of talking too much, of falling into monologue. John Sculley was president of Apple Computer and responsible for developing the company in the face of enormous competition. He made it a huge success. Once he was interviewed by CNN and was asked about his job description. He replied, "I am Chief Listener."

One of the best listeners in my circle of friends is a successful businessman who in the space of two decades quietly built a commercial empire with a current annual turnover of several billion dollars. I had the privilege of working closely with him for several years. Although his calendar was always full of appointments, outwardly he never appeared pressed for time. I remember several meetings in which he listened for hours on end with rapt attention while apparently trifling matters were described in detail. I am convinced that this ability is one of the key ingredients to his success.

What is active listening?

Active listening involves a readiness to see things from other people's viewpoints and to empathize with their feelings.

Equally necessary is an awareness of our tendency to "tune out" or "go on automatic," which is not listening at all. This tendency can be controlled by concentrating on understanding what the other person says and excluding personal thoughts. A good tip is to take notes while the other person talks.

Here are some tips to help you listen actively:

❏ Look at the other person attentively. I don't mean that you should stare, but looking into his or her eyes and nodding whenever something important has been said are aids to active listening. Do not feel that you must repeat every point made to you. Paraphrase only the important factual or emotional statements that you think need to be confirmed. This encourages full disclosure.

❏ Ask questions to clarify a statement. Don't overdo it, but ask from time to time if you understood the other person's remarks correctly. Asking for clarification provides the other person with the opportunity to determine whether he or she has been correctly understood.

❏ Use the classical body language for listening: tilt your head, look at the other person, and show interest on your face.

Although active listening is a difficult and tiring job, the necessary skills can be learned quite easily. It does, however, require complete concentration.

Through active listening you find out more

If you like the person you are talking to, you should be interested in listening to what he has to say. Listening provides the best opportunity to get to know the personality and hidden agenda of your partner. To listen means to immerse yourself, to depart from your own standpoint, to follow the other's train of thought, to absorb his forms of expression and body language, to try to understand him as a whole. If you are properly immersed in a conversation or negotiation, you have little time for preparing your next intervention.

Have you ever seen the concentration a child puts into listening to a story? Body, eyes, facial expression, breathing – everything is geared to listening. If you listen in this way, you'll be surprised at what you find out. Your discussion partner will reveal an extraordinary amount through the intellectual construction of an argument, through choice of words, through intensity of gestures. All you have to do is learn how to "read" him properly.

You should pay special attention when you meet someone who has the ability to really listen. You are likely dealing with someone who knows how to "see with the ears" and who uses this capacity quite consciously and purposefully.

The big secret to effective listening: pauses

What do skilled listeners use as their secret weapon? Pauses. Pausing may sound simple, but in fact it is a real test of patience that is not easy to master. Our biggest obstacle is our own need for recognition. Who wants to always listen to others? We, too, want to introduce our own great thoughts on the subject. We, too, want to be taken seriously. But if both conversationalists adopt this attitude, the conversation will disintegrate into empty, disjointed chatter that has little to do with sincere dialogue. To break this cycle, see to it that you are the first to start really listening.

How can you learn to listen?

The best listening techniques don't require you never to speak. On the contrary, listening is an intensive psychological process of immersing yourself in another person's psyche, a creative achievement of the highest order.

First, set yourself a goal to ask one or two opening questions – and then say no more. The other person will answer the questions and then fall into silence. You should also remain silent, even if the pause drags out over a considerable time. You should use body language to display great interest in your partner's opinion and to silently encourage her to go on talking. Use the classic listening signals, such as an interested facial expression, head to one side, upper body leaning forward. At first you may feel as if your body language is slightly forced, but you soon will become quite comfortable with it.

Now you will discover something important. Through your silence you are indicating to the other person that you are tuned in to her and that you are ready to receive her ideas with interest. All this has an extremely positive effect. When she starts to speak, she may repeat her first answer, worded differently, expressed more candidly, more openly, and more honestly. Her speech will flow more freely and more directly. Keep the discussion going by feeding just enough fuel to keep the fire smoldering. Ask short questions or ask for examples, but be careful not to summarize the answers or offer opinions. If you guard against commenting on or supplementing the answers with a sparkling brilliant idea of your own, your partner's comments will draw to a close. Put yourself in the other person's shoes and you will be amazed at the information you receive.

Try it out. Practice and test these methods with friends, colleagues, and family. Let the other person have his say, even if he sometimes struggles to find words. If you intervene, do so only with information questions, then relapse into silence; the other person may have a belated thought he wants to add. Now that you are not thinking of what to say next, you can devote that extra time to following the line of discussion. Consider his motivation, what weight he gives to certain points, whether there are contradictions in what he says, whether his body language coincides with his verbal message, and what emotional effect certain words have on you. You may even wonder how and why you would have discussed the topic in a different way.

You may feel that you could never stop yourself from talking as your own temperament will prove an insurmountable obstacle. Just think about weightlifters. They must start off with small weights and practice, practice, practice every day. When eventually they lift up mighty weights with apparent ease, this is the final result of unrelenting attention to detail, ever more strenuous practice, and great strength of mind. In the same way, you can learn to listen to others. At the start of your training, you will experience moderate success. Soon you will be able to listen for longer and longer periods. Gradually it will become comfortable and routine.

Listen intently and the results will astonish you. Sadly, in today's fast-paced world, most people feel that their thoughts and ideas are rarely heard or given any weight. People are grateful if someone suddenly listens to them, not only taking them seriously but even wanting to hear more. All this bears results. The other person will open up to you and will probably tell you more than he had originally intended because he has developed a rapport with you. Without being pressured, the information he gives you is honest, undiluted, and direct.

This does not mean that the skill of listening cannot be misused. I have met people who make a sport out of listening without interruption, asking only very specific questions if they want to extract more information. It doesn't take long before this has a counterproductive effect, with their conversation partners feeling they are insincere, if not cunning and deceptive.

The psychology of listening

Bookstore shelves are stacked with dozens of advice manuals recommending the everyday application of psychology. Listening is also an important psychological tool, but I do not believe that the technique of listening used in psychoanalysis is suitable for normal communication in business and private life. If you are familiar with this method, whether from a self-help organization, one-on-one counseling, or classical Freudian psychoanalysis, there may be a great temptation to carry this method into everyday application. I advise against it.

In psychoanalysis, for example, the personal emotions of the patient are transferred to the listening analyst. These transferences are part of the healing process. They enable the patient to relive his problems under controlled conditions. This way he can reconsider them and reach an adequate solution to them. In one-to-one counseling, on the other hand, transference plays no part. Here the therapist concentrates on the feelings the patient only partly outlines. Through listening techniques, the therapist enables the patient to define these emotions, acknowledging and understanding them.

What do you do if the other person is so delighted to have a genuine listener that she never stops talking? This may be hard to believe, but you will hardly ever run into this problem. A genuine listener attracts sympathy and awakens the other person's sense of fairness. I have found again and again that after a certain amount of time, the roles are reversed and the other person listens with the same avid interest as you did. Genuine listening is infectious. Try it!

Summing up

Talking and listening really belong together, like two sides of a coin. This chapter showed the unexpected insights you can gain merely by learning how to listen properly. And don't forget the number-one secret: insert pauses into the flow of conversation.

Chapter 12

The power of body language

Do you remember Walt Disney's delightful short cartoons? The spoken word was of no importance. The cartoon characters communicated to us almost entirely in body movements. Mickey's radiance or the incredulous, astonished expression on Goofy's face spoke more than a thousand words.

"**S**he speaks with her hands." "It felt like he saw right through me." "The eyes are the windows to the soul." These common expressions illustrate that the body has its own language. We transmit a constant flow of signals in the way we sit, stand, walk, and talk. The effect these signals have on the subconscious is what we sometimes refer to as a person's aura.

The deciphering of non-verbal signals is an area that lays itself open to much misinterpretation. Special care is required when interpreting body language, since false conclusions can adversely affect our aim of getting what we want. Deciphering body language is a journey into the unknown, with a high probability of misreading the situation, as the following little anecdote shows.

An entire office staff was working on a big contract worth millions of dollars, and preparations for the proposal kept everyone on the move. Finally, the last decisive meeting arrived. The members of the negotiating team were tense as they awaited the final cost discussion. The sales manager had even undergone a course in body language so as to be able to read the secret thoughts of the buyer and unhesitatingly make the appropriate response.

After the usual preliminaries, the moment came when they named their price: $12.5 million. At just that moment, the facial expression of the buyer changed: he looked away, leaned back, crossed his legs, and appeared uneasy. The leader of the delegation read this reaction as surprise at the price and went on smoothly, "...and because it's a first order we can allow a new customer a discount of four percent."

An agreement was made and the business was done. For years afterwards, the sales manager boasted that they had his cunning knowledge of body language and his speedy reaction to thank for their success.

Much later, I heard the other side of this story. The buyer felt very good about the contract and was willing to spend what it took to get it done right. But at the very instant the two parties began to talk about the price, he realized he needed to go to the bathroom. He had no objection to the price, he only wanted to put the conversation on hold for a short time so he could take a quick break. This was the only reason he changed his position. For a long time afterwards he rejoiced at the fact that his discomfort had saved his company half a million dollars.

If you are expecting me to give you instructions on how to

read unconscious body signals in order to detect the hidden motives of your partner, I'm going to disappoint you. Because of the great risk of misunderstandings, the interpretation of body language holds no major significance in the art of getting what we want. There are a number of good books on the subject and you can easily develop your knowledge in this direction. However, I believe the risk of misinterpretation outweighs the useful information you may glean in this way.

Concealing our emotions

We frequently wear a mask. People have become expert at controlling their bodies and hiding their feelings. Many may even deliberately use false body language to trick other people. Unfortunately there is no sure way of differentiating between real and false body signals.

What does it mean when someone holds his head at an angle during a conversation or speech? We generally assume the person is listening attentively. Public speakers watch the way members of the audience are holding their heads to check whether they are "getting through" or whether they need to alter the presentation. The same is true during conversation. But what if the listener deliberately holds her head to the side, to create a false impression? She may not be listening at all but preparing her next statement.

The risks in reading body language

There are no absolutely certain signals in body language. This fact alone should stand as a warning to us, for there is nothing more dangerous than misinterpreted signals.

Reading body language correctly is a tricky business. Every signal can have at least two interpretations. How do you know which one is correct? What does it mean when the person you are talking to leans forward? Does it signify an inclination to listen or does it simply express a wish to better hear what is being said?

Misinterpretations are dangerous

Get accustomed to watching for subtle differences between fiction and reality. Anyone who observes politicians during an election campaign will become aware of this discrepancy quickly. Politicians are often good actors, and with the help of an image consultant they can present a picture quite far from reality. Once the politician is elected, off comes the mask, and he rarely again ever presents himself as stylishly as he did during the campaign. Most of us realize this, so it is all the more astonishing that we continue to let ourselves be impressed by meaningless gestures.

Advertising works in exactly the same way. Here body language is indisputably artificial and false. For toothpaste ads, an actor dresses up as a dentist; for detergent ads, a model poses as the average homemaker.

Of course, this does not mean you should pay no attention to the person you are talking to. However, it is not as important to decipher exactly what signals are being unconsciously emitted, as to determine at which point in the conversation the other person changes his or her demeanor.

For example, it is not important to observe whether someone smokes and how he holds the cigarette, but it *might* be important to notice at which moment he lights up or stubs out. This might indicate that the topic you have reached has some importance to him. Likewise, it is of no importance that someone doodles matchstick people, or where on the page, or what kind of matchstick people, but it is of significance at what moment she starts or stops scribbling. This could indicate a higher state of alertness, but then again, it also could indicate boredom.

Be careful. By trying to decipher body language you are entering a field of speculation, which can easily lead to wrong assumptions and threaten your efforts.

Speaking of body language, allow me to add one more point and look at the other side of the picture: you. If you have to appear on TV or in any other public function, your body language is extremely important. If there is a discrepancy between what you say verbally and how you communicate your language with your body, it could have a negative effect, putting your credibility at risk. If you ever have to appear on TV or speak in public, you must seek some advice on how to present yourself.

But taking lessons or getting a wardrobe consultant is not enough. You have to believe in what you do. In seminars, you will learn how to present yourself, but don't accept everything you're taught. For instance, you might learn in such seminars never to put your hands in your pocket, not to slouch, always to stress certain words, or even, if the audience expects this, to roll up your sleeves, undo the top button of your shirt, and loosen your tie. But be careful. Every one of your gestures, every gesticulation, every signal has to be in synch with your personality. If they are not, you will not be credible. Audiences will figure it out.

Summing up

I am not offering a course in deciphering body language, as it is not an exact science and often leads to dangerous false conclusions. But remember, it is not as important what someone does as when he does it. The most important thing is for you to be credible all the time.

Step Five

Don't Take No For an Answer!

Step One	Get the Right Information
Step Two	Investigate Motives
Step Three	Ask the Right Questions / Give the Right Answers
Step Four	Listen Actively
Step Five	Don't Take No for an Answer!

Chapter 13

No means maybe

Two employees of a shoe factory were sent by their director to Africa to investigate the possibilities of opening up a branch office. One wrote in his report, "Nothing doing, here they all go barefoot." His colleague began with the words, "Huge potential..."

Do you take no for an answer? This chapter is perhaps the most important in this book. Most attempts to get our own way fail because we have accepted no as a final answer. Far too often a no is accepted without challenge.

Strike the word "no" from your vocabulary. It's such a small word, yet it causes so much conflict. If you avoid using it unless absolutely necessary, you may be able to get to the point where a no is never spoken. And if it still happens on occasion? Don't get upset. Stay focused and try to convert this no into a maybe and then into a yes. In this chapter, you will learn this art of changing a no into a yes.

There are really only two rules to observe as far as the unwelcome no is concerned:

❑ Never break the line of communication

❑ Avoid having the word "no" spoken in the first place

Never break the lines of communication

Whatever may happen during the course of negotiation, take care that the bridge of communication never breaks between you and your partner. Even when facing the toughest opposition, you should ensure that a channel of communication remains open. This doesn't need to be a six-lane superhighway; a minor suspension bridge will do. Even a narrow rope will help in cases of emergency. I have had excellent results with the following tactic:

When negotiating a price, I never ask, "Will you give a discount?" I always ask, "How much is your discount?"

And if the answer is no, I reply with a smile, "Is this a big no or a small no?"

What do I mean by leaving the lines of communication open? I mean discussing shared interests and common bonds. This should be fairly simple to do as people always have things in common. Besides establishing common ground and getting to know your partner, remember these connecting threads when the going gets tough. If you have skillfully introduced these common interests during the original set up of negotiations, you should be able to renew that bond later, even when circumstances have changed. And situations are continually changing, often in unforeseen ways.

Even states at war keep channels of communication open through the good services of third parties. Why shouldn't we use this custom that has developed over the centuries? For examples and further suggestions as to how you can alter situations, review Chapter 3, Winners Create a Good Atmosphere.

Avoid having the word "no" spoken in the first place

Once the other person has uttered the word "no," he has taken a stance. It will not be easy to change his mind, especially if it means he will lose face. It would be dangerous for him to compromise his credibility and reputation.

The key to avoiding a no answer is asking only open-ended questions. This way the response cannot be no. Here are a few situations to consider:

(a) *You arrive at the wine store just as the staff is closing up for the night. If you ask, "Can I still buy something?" you will receive an immediate no from the sales assistant. It's far better to say, "I really need a bottle of wine. Here's the exact amount of money." This way you avoided receiving a "no" and have generated action. Another way would be to ask the question, "Could you help me, please?"*

(b) *As a sales associate in a jewelry store you are serving a customer who seems to like a certain ring. She says, "I'll only buy it if I get a 20 percent discount." If you answer, "No, I can't do that," the sale will be in doubt. Instead, avoid a direct answer by saying, "We'll go into the question of a discount later, but have you noticed that..." Or "That could be difficult, but I think we can come to some terms. Look here..." By directing attention back to the ring you can avoid answering with a direct no and getting a no in return. You keep the discussion and interest going.*

What to do, if despite everything, no is spoken

When I was renovating my kitchen, I contacted a kitchen specialist who had been recommended to me. His first (and only) question was, "When do you want it finished by?" When I told him that it had to be ready for use within eight weeks, he emphatically replied that it was impossible for him and terminated the discussion. He did

not question me about my deadline or offer any expla-
nations. He not only lost that contract but any future
work from me and of course my referrals. He'll only find
out about his loss by reading this book. He never con-
tacted me again.

In a case like the above there is no point in challenging the
no, and it's best to leave it at that. When you receive a firm,
final no, there is nothing left for you to do except take a step
back and wait for the atmosphere to improve. You can then
return to tackle the matter from a different angle, but there will
be a loss of time and energy that could have been avoided.

But in most cases, if you want to get your way, you simply cannot accept no for an answer. If you get a weak no, you
can simply ignore it. The other person will be unlikely to
protest against a subsequent comment, such as, "I want to
add something…" or, with a smile, "I didn't quite get your
no. Is it perhaps…"

No seems so harmless

Why does the little word "no" have so much power? Because it
appears mostly in disguise. We would do well to become
acquainted with the various guises that bestow such exceptional influence on this little word.

The trivial no

This is the trivial no that we run into every day. If you ask a
waiter if he has unsweetened iced tea and he says, "Sorry, we
don't have any," that is a no. It's not worth wasting any thought
on such a no. You will just order something else and the matter will be settled. Sometimes there is no point in wanting to get
your own way.

The emotional no

The no spoken in annoyance, anger, or rage is usually rash and should be avoided. Later, when the anger is spent and reason has returned, you may think better of it. The problem is, if your pride is wounded, you may stubbornly maintain your position, often at a very high price. Now you really have made matters worse, for you run the risk of losing your credibility.

Here are a few examples of emotional nos that it would better to avoid.

- ❏ In the context of divorce: "I *never* want to see you again."

- ❏ Raising a child: "If you do that one more time…"

- ❏ When shopping: "I'll *never* step foot inside your store again."

A couple had just booked into a hotel in Las Vegas. They paid for the night and wanted to make a long-distance telephone call out of the country from their room. The hotel telephone operator refused to make the connection unless they paid for the call cash in advance.

That was too much for our uptight couple. They took their complaint right up the ladder from the operator to the manager. The hotel staff remained friendly and cordial while explaining that these measures, which applied to all, had been taken because of bad experiences with previous guests. The staff affirmed their present guests' creditworthiness and the validity of their credit card, but still insisted that they pay in advance.

The poor guests' rage grew until finally they left the hotel as a protest, despite having already paid for their room and getting no refund. They then spent hours searching for alternative accommodation.

This couple wanted to get their own way and asserted their "rights," but at what cost! The tourists paid dearly for this.

The elegantly packaged no

This no comes across in a friendly, aloof manner, usually presented in a hard-to-catch way. It is difficult to overcome.

Banks are notorious for double-speak and confusion. In this example, an oversight by the bank delayed a remittance resulting in a loss. The customer demanded compensation. The bank's reply took the following form:

We acknowledge with great interest your written communication and we are extremely sorry for the error. We would first like to thank you sincerely for taking the time to draw our attention to the problem. This will enable us to inspect and improve our internal working practices. By informing us of the situation, you were acting in the interest of our other customers as well. We can understand your annoyance at the incident and your feeling that you are entitled to compensation. Unfortunately, although we would be delighted to grant your request, we are not empowered to do so, as the Bank Act regulations forbid us to pay damages for mistakes leading to delays of fewer than eight working days beyond a deadline, even if the mistakes are attributable directly or indirectly to our organization...

The bank has packaged its no into a stylish but empty flow of words. Such bureaucratic replies can run to two or three pages all the while elegantly saying a great big no.

The no in yes disguise

Your partner may disguise his no by saying yes, but behave in such a way that he obviously means no.

> *You invite someone out for lunch who says yes but because of a "full calendar of appointments" won't commit himself. He promises to call you back but never does. If this happens several times, it is a clear message: a definite no, albeit in disguise.*

I know a family who holds an open house a few times a year. They issue a constant stream of invitations. Whoever turns them down is invited again at the next opportunity. Three refusals are taken as a lack of interest and the person is never invited again. A good system.

When you say no

So far, we have concentrated on refusals from your partner in a negotiation. There are, however, situations where you have to give no for an answer. You need to select the form of no appropriate to what you wish to achieve. If you are using no as a form of strategy, perhaps to gain time, you might try "no, not at the moment…" If your goal is to put an end to all further discussion, you should choose the firm no. You will use this no, for example, if you find that after a long round of negotiations, the other person insists on getting approval from a higher authority, when you were under the impression that they had the final say. You must not let such a trick go by without comment. Your no might be a statement in which you claim the same right to treat the decision as not binding and subject to change.

Just as we wish to continue negotiations with our partners, even when they give us a no, your own no must be flexible. If you tailor your no to the situation and use flexible wording, should the situation change, all avenues still remain open to you.

When checking into a hotel in Switzerland I was confronted with an unusually detailed form to fill in, requesting a lot of personal information. I thought this was bureaucratic nonsense and said so. Every single one of my arguments met with the same angelically patient response, "It's company policy, sir." A few weeks later, to my surprise, the forms were dispensed with. When I inquired about it, the terse answer was, "The company policy has changed."

The firmer the no, the gentler the words

Let's assume you have to fire an employee – a message that is, in effect, a no. Regardless of the reason for dismissal, it will come as a heavy blow and therefore should be conveyed in a gentle way. There are various methods of doing this, from a formal letter to a personal heart-to-heart conversation. Your choice will often depend not so much on your personal preference as on external circumstances. The wording should be gentle, causing as little pain as possible to the other party.

I once applied for a job I wanted very much. Accordingly, I spent much time and energy in trying to secure the position. Unfortunately, it didn't work out. I can't recall the reason for the rejection, but to this day the format it took remains clear in my mind. The letter began with the following words, "Unfortunately, I have to tell you that the job has gone to another applicant. Now that I have broken the bad news, I am free to tell you that I rated your application very highly."

The rest of the letter was a positive, thoughtfully word-ed commentary on me and my career to date. The letter closed with the hope that I would understand the com-pany's necessity of making a choice.

There is no standard formula for turning a no into a maybe. You have to choose the method according to the situation and must be prepared to change whenever the circumstances change. Two ideal qualities to possess are creativity and tenacity while never losing sight of your goal.

There are many books and courses aimed at honing your creativity in negotiation and communication. I recommend one book in particular, *Stratagems*. The dictionary defines the word "stratagem" as "a war maneuver, trick." The author of this book, Harry von Senger, a lawyer and sinologist, studied this subject for years in China and Japan and wrote more than 400 pages filled with tactics and maneuvers. Although they origi-nate in the culture of the Far East, they can be adapted to some degree to our own use.

An example from the book, in my own words:

The mayor of a provincial capital in China discovered that the official seal of his district was missing. Due to an impending visit by the provincial governor it was important to find the seal quickly. The mayor was almost certain that the prison warden was responsible for the theft, but he had no proof. He enlisted the services of someone well-versed in stratagems who promised to get the seal back within three days. During the third night, fire broke out in the civic building. Everyone hurried to the site to help put out the flames. When Hu, the prison warden, arrived the mayor handed him the closed box that usually contained the seal and asked him to look after it and keep it safe from the fire. The warden saw the light and realized he had fallen into a trap. If the box had been opened after the fire and it was discovered the seal was missing, the warden would have been blamed and punished. When the mayor opened the box the next day, the seal once again lay safely inside.

Summing up

This chapter demonstrates how a no can be converted into a maybe and then into a yes without causing any hurt to the opposite party. Never forget the two rules: (a) never break the lines of communication and (b) avoid having the word "no" spoken in the first place. And remember: Don't ever accept no for an answer!

And Keep
in Mind

Chapter 14

Frequently asked questions

The following questions are asked as people begin negotiating the way this book teaches. I believe the best answers will become clearer when you begin to put it all together. Getting what you want is not an exact science, and sometimes there is more than one valid response to a situation. I have answered the questions in the way that is right for me. You will, of course, come up with different answers. I have no objection to this; on the contrary, I welcome you to take a critical look at my answers, as you must operate using *your* style, *your* method, and *your* way of working.

Q: Are there any rules about when a negotiation should take place?

A: You won't always get the chance to decide the time, but if you can, then by all means go ahead. Make the arrangements for a time when you are at your peak performance level. If you are not a morning person, it would be best to meet after lunch. Or do you tend to get tired toward midday and are lethargic after lunch? Then earlier in the day would be more suitable. Try to plan the agenda to suit your own biorhythms.

Q: Who should I deal with?

A: It's not always easy to find the appropriate person. If you enter in at too high a point in the hierarchy you might offend the official who should have been dealing with your matter and arouse his or her hostility. However, if you concentrate your efforts on someone too low on the pole, they may shelve the problem with the notorious, "I'm not allowed to make such a decision on my own." It's worth your while to establish clearly the appropriate level for your negotiations.

Q: How do I prepare myself for an important meeting?

A: Collect as much background information as possible, regardless of whether or not you may use it. Another necessary part of preparation is psyching yourself up to deal with any tricky situation. You need to be calm and well prepared. Temporarily avoid anything that conflicts with the pursuit of your agenda. You should try to adapt to your partner's style and to foresee any problems so that when they crop up in conversation you won't be taken by surprise.

Q: How important is the location of a meeting?

A: In general, it can be very important if it helps to calm you or put you on neutral ground. Location is normally decided by the inviting party. If you can choose the place, pick a spot where you feel secure, whether your own office or a neutral territory such as a restaurant. Show up at the restaurant at least 10 minutes early so that you can choose a table and determine a strategically favorable seat.

Q: At meetings, I always get bogged down in details. What am I doing wrong?

A: I would guess that you take no active part in leading the conversation and allow yourself to drift into chit-chat. Instead, make up your mind not to delve into details irrelevant to the business at hand. For example, deal briefly with excuses for being late or for misunderstandings and then go straight on to other matters. This will tighten the course of negotiation.

Q: If both parties are completely adamant and are not willing to compromise, what are my chances of breaking the stalemate?

A: Try the following: Call in a neutral third party respected by both sides. It will not be easy to find such a person, but if one can be found and agrees to act as intermediary, there is an excellent chance of reaching a reasonable solution. You might want to try to find a professional mediator. Sometimes results can be obtained by changing the location of the meeting, bringing in an expert, etc. Take one step back now in order to be able to take two steps forward at a later point.

Make the first move. Let your opponent know you feel the situation has taken a turn for the worse and that this is not what you want. Then suggest, for example, an unofficial meeting or a short telephone conversation. Be careful that this behavior is not construed as a sign of weakness. If there is any danger of this, don't do it.

Q: How do I practice taking control of conversations?

A: The following is a difficult but effective exercise. During a social discussion with friends, try to bring the topic of conversation around to a particular theme, for example, the signs of the zodiac or skiing, without the others noticing. At first, you will have little success in diverting the flow of conversation inconspicuously, but it is an outstanding exercise for learning to lead discussions.

Q: What do you suggest about appropriate dress?

A: Dress in such a way that it doesn't become an issue. Wear whatever blends in with the other side. If you feel the need to comment on some item of your attire, for example, your reason for not wearing a tie, then something is wrong. Avoid flaunting status symbols unless this is part of your plan.

Q: Is what you describe here not simply a particularly clever form of manipulation?

A: No, quite the contrary. Nowhere in the entire book does the word "manipulation" occur, and that is deliberate. The dictionary defines manipulation as "conscious and purposeful influence upon people without their knowledge and often against their will." I utterly deplore this kind of influence. This aversion was one of my original reasons for writing the book. Our awareness of such methods evens up the odds and gives the manipulators less of an opportunity.

Chapter 15

Some case studies

This chapter contains several case studies and detailed commentary to show you how the five steps that get you to yes can be put to use. I have chosen examples from the business world, but the five steps can also help you resolve situations in your everyday private life.

Good luck with your negotiations, and remember, you will achieve the best results if your actions are not directed by emotions like anger or frustration. You should only proceed when your anger is under control. And your reaction should be entirely goal-oriented.

Case study #1

Meet David Huntington, 65 years old, retired

David Huntington signed up for the American Express Platinum credit card because American Express was offering a free companion airline ticket for every airline ticket purchased with the card. David, a retired executive who liked to travel, would pay for his ticket and American Express would give him a free ticket for his wife. This seemed like an interesting and attractive promotion. David paid the yearly fee of $399 and was looking forward to his text trip.

But a few months later, when David was ready to order his tickets, he was told that the companion ticket promotion was no longer offered by American Express.

David sent an email to American Express's Customer Service department asking for an explanation. This is the answer he received:

Thank you for your recent email. Unfortunately, at this time a replacement for the Companion Ticket program has not been confirmed. However, we are diligently working at resolving this issue and will try to provide you with an answer in the future. We appreciate your concern, time and patience in this matter.

David decided to give them a second chance and sent them another email:

Sorry, I cannot accept your answer. Although I am happy to hear that you are "diligently working at resolving this issue," you did not answer my question. Here is the text of my question again:

"It was about six months ago when I signed up for the Platinum card. The main reason for joining was your offer of one free airplane ticket worldwide if another one was purchased with the card. Shortly afterwards I discovered that this service was discontinued. Please let me know what I can do to use the service that was promised."

I am not willing to accept an answer that contains nothing but banalities. This is not an easy matter for me and it shouldn't be for you. You made a promise and didn't keep it. That is what matters.

Here is the reply he received from American Express:

Thank you for your recent email and feedback. Unfortunately at this time we cannot provide you with an exact date. We appreciate your time and patience in this matter.

What would you do now? Would you fight or let it go? If the former, *how* would you fight? Read on to see what David did.

David's response

Angered by the automated, cliché-ridden response, David decided to storm the barricades, using the five steps in *Don't Take No for an Answer!* at least to get his registration fee back.

His first step was to get information. He called the American Express switchboard, told them that he had to write a letter to the CEO, and got his full name and address. Then he had someone else call to get the name of the person responsible for Amercian Express's credit card department. Next he did a search on the Internet and found out that a class-action suit for breach of contract was filed against American Express regarding exactly the same matter. That made him feel better and gave him confidence.

With this information in hand, David proceeded to the next step, aiming as high as possible. He wrote a letter to the person responsible for the Visa department and copied the CEO. Here are some passages from this letter:

> *I am writing to you personally and would like to bring the following matter to your attention. As a business owner I understand the importance and profitability associated with loyal customers. I have been trying to build a loyal relationship with your company as a Platinum card member. However, an event has just occurred that threatens this loyalty.*

After describing what happened, he continued:

> *I have contacted the responsible parties through normal channels but have been rebuffed and blocked. This is why I am asking for your intervention. To restore my confidence in your company, I expect that the issue with the companion ticket will be resolved to my satisfaction or the fee of $399 will be refunded.*

David's letter was answered by an assistant. The response – a whole page this time – was a flat unspoken no. The letter was a masterpiece of talking around an issue and saying nothing in 443 words (I counted them). It is worth quoting from:

> *It is apparent that we failed to provide you with all of the information relative to the "replacement" of this unique benefit ... Based on the circumstances we certainly understand how you may feel ... We regret if this recent incident caused any concern or embarrassment for yourself ... We genuinely hope that this most unfortunate experience has not entirely jeopardized our fine relationship and we look forward to many more years of pleasant problem-free association ....*

In spite of all the eloquent words, they weren't budging a bit.

What now? Many people would have given up. David Huntington did not.

He did more research on the Internet and found out that American Express had an ombudswoman who worked exclusively for their organization. He contacted her and after a couple of weeks he received a letter telling him he was right and apologizing for the way he was treated. The $399 was immediately refunded.

Comments

Did David Huntington follow the five steps?

He followed Step One, Get the Right Information, but missed the fact that an ombudswoman was available at American Express. If he had known this at the beginning, he could have skipped all the correspondence and sent his request directly to her.

He could have done more with Step Two, Investigate Motives, and realized that the CEO of such a large organization was hardly likely to get in touch with a small client. Having said that, the picture would probably have changed if he had played the card of his knowledge of the class-action suit.

As there was no verbal communication, he correctly eliminated Step Three, Ask the Right Questions/Give the Right Answers, and Step Four, Listen Actively.

David followed the most important one, Step Five, Don't Take No for an Answer, refusing to give up after receiving negative answers from American Express.

Was is worth it?

Calculated purely on the basis of cost and revenue it might not have been worth the time and all the aggravation for $399, but for David Huntington, an important moral issue was at stake. He was proud of the fact that he always honored the commitments he made in his life and just couldn't let any corporation get away with – as he said called it – such a misuse of power.

In my opinion a very valid point.

Case study #2

Meet Doreen Tuttle, a 25-year-old secretary

Doreen bought an IBM laptop computer for $2,500 from a small store. She paid cash, took it home, and put it to use right away. Two days later, while reading the newspaper, she discovered an advertisement from the same store offering exactly the same model for $1,950.

She immediately called the store and asked for her money back. But the salesperson would not cooperate. Digging his heels in, he refused to give her a refund, pointing to the fact that their business had been finalized before the price cut was offered. He also asked her if she hadn't seen the sign: "All sales final." Case closed.

If you were Doreen Tuttle, what would you do now? How would you react?

Doreen's response

Doreen telephoned another IBM dealer and made a general inquiry about a computer. Directing the conversation to the issue of the price cut, she learned that the cut was initiated by IBM itself. She received the date when the sale had started and realized that it was exactly one day after her own purchase.

Then Doreen called IBM directly and asked for help with her problem. The sales manager informed her that he had no power to influence the sales policy of independent stores but that he considered the shop in question to be reputable.

As the discussion went along, Doreen found out two important details. She learned that IBM offered stock protection for the special. This meant, explained the sales manager, that IBM would make good the difference between the old price and the reduced price on the inventory the shop had in stock. And she also learned that the computer shop where she made her purchase was owned by a gentleman by the name of Jack McKay. Doreen thanked the sales manager for his help and offered to keep him informed about the further course of events.

As direct action had achieved nothing, Doreen decided to write a letter to the owner of the computer shop:

Dear Mr. McKay,

On August 31, I bought an IBM computer in your shop and paid $2,500 in cash. (Enclosed is a copy of the receipt.) The next day, I read in a newspaper that you were offering the same model for $1,950. In my opinion, your company should refund the difference of $550 to me.

You enjoy an excellent reputation, and that is by no means always the case in the computer business. This image has been built up over the years by impeccable business conduct, as was confirmed to me, incidentally, by a third party. This is my reason for approaching you directly.

Would you not also think it unfair if your supplier still charged you the old, higher price the very day before the price came down? Besides, you've got the changeover period to work with, because IBM informed me that with their stock protection in force, in my case they would cover you for the difference in relation to the new retail price. You would therefore suffer no loss.

I look forward to hearing from you and will be happy if in the future I can continue to recommend your business.

Yours sincerely,

Doreen Tuttle

cc IBM

Two weeks later Doreen Tuttle received a check for $550 in the mail. She wrote a quick thank-you note to Mr. McKay for dealing so positively with her inquiry and also informed the IBM sales manager. The matter was closed satisfactorily for everyone concerned.

Comments

Did Doreen Tuttle follow the five steps?

Yes, she did. She did an excellent job in Step One, Get the Right Information, by calling a competitor and getting information from him, and then she got lucky getting the important information about stock protection from the IBM sales manager. I am not sure if he was entitled to give her that crucial information but it shows Doreen's talent in listening actively (Step Four) and asking the right questions (Step Three). It was also a good move to tell him that she would keep him informed about further developments. This allowed her to give her letter more weight.

As for Step Five, Don't Take No for an Answer!, she lived up to its essence, that no means maybe, and worded the letter to the dealer in such a way that his interest was at the forefront. Doreen did not write "I feel I have been cheated" or "I want my money back." Instead she turned the tables around by asking the dealer how he would feel in a similar situation. An excellent move. She also inserted a compliment about the store's reputation and intentionally made no mention of the unfortunate conversation with the computer salesman. The inclusion of a "copy to IBM" indicated that she had been in touch with them.

What can we learn from Doreen Tuttle?

In spite of the rude rebuff from the salesperson, Doreen remained calm. She did not let her anger dominate her. She also did not disclose her plan of action, in order to prevent the salesman from sabotaging her efforts. She let him believe that the matter was closed. And she worded her letter to the owner in such a way that he had practically no choice but to refund her. Doreen did an excellent job and got her money back with little effort.

Case study #3

Meet Dr. Philip Evans, successful entrepreneur

Dr. Evans always uses his Visa credit card in order to accumulate air miles for his travels. Ten days before a planned trip to Europe he ordered two tickets and told Visa to transfer 200,000 air miles to his account with British Airways.

Being the detail-oriented person that he was, he asked again two days later. He was told that the transfer was in progress. After another two days, when the miles still hadn't arrived at BA, he called again and asked what happened. "Not to worry. Everything is under control," was the answer. But the air miles hadn't arrived a week later and when he called Visa again he was informed that the miles were refused by British Airways because the Frequent Flyer number didn't match their records.

Dr. Evans double-checked the number – he had given the correct one, and there was no doubt that the mistake had been made by Visa.

Panicking, he called Visa daily, but received no help. The people he dealt with were completely uninterested, and when he asked for a supervisor he was put on hold for half an hour before being connected. He told the supervisor that he risked losing his ticket. Her answer was, "I am sorry but that is your problem; there is nothing I can do."

After over a dozen more phone calls to Visa and British Airways, Dr. Evans finally found a helpful operator, but by then it was too late. One day before his planned travel date, the tickets could not be issued as the deadline had passed. He had to cancel the trip.

How would you react if you were in his shoes?

Dr. Evans's response

Dr. Evans was furious and wanted to sue Visa for having caused great damage. And he also wanted to inform the media and the public of his unacceptable experience with the company.

The next morning he was still furious but had a little more perspective. He realized that the actions he had planned the day before would have been dictated by anger. It would have been a long and difficult process and would not have compensated him for the costs related to the cancellation.

So, using the five steps, he got the names of the important people and wrote an explanatory letter, delivering it personally. The letter contained a detailed report of what happened, with all the names he could remember. He did not forget to praise the helpful customer-service person in Vancouver.

Twenty-four hours later he received a phone call from the head of the Visa department. She thanked him for his letter, apologized for what happened, and offered him two first-class tickets to Europe for free.

Not only did he accept, he also wrote a letter of thanks to all the recipients of the first letter, telling them how grateful he was for their quick and satisfactory solution and indicating that he would be happy to continue doing business with Visa.

What can we learn from Dr. Evans?

It is always good to put some distance between your intial feelings of anger and your response. This will give you time to decide if you want to react at all or if you should let it go. If you decide to react, your steps should be purely goal-oriented, and not influenced by emotions.

As a result of Dr. Evans's response, the CEO of the corporation decided to completely reorganize that department and make it more user-friendly, which was in the interest of the bank and future clients. Dr. Evans's reaction had a dramatic and positive effect not only for himself but also for others.

An interesting detail: In his letter, Dr. Evans asked for a specific compensation – air miles for two free tickets – which gave his letter some credibility because he set a parameter and communicated to the other party what he expected. It is not always wise to do that, because you don't want to limit your expectations, but in this case it seems to me that it was right.

Following is the text of Dr. Evans' letter.

Dear Sir,

I am writing to you to express my extreme frustration with the complete lack of customer service that I had to experience from the staff of your Visa department which led to the last minute cancellation of my business trip. This cancellation will have severe consequences.

I am angry not because a mistake occurred, but because no one in a long chain of employees of your credit card department – with one exception – showed any interest in assisting me to correct that mistake. The opposite is true: your staff was completely un-cooperative and I was continually treated with indifference, contempt, and a failure to recognize or resolve the problem.

I am attaching a detailed summary that will give you the necessary information.

The last-minute cancellation of my business trip was not only an inconvenience, it has had severe consequences, as you can imagine. I have been forced to reschedule multiple meetings that had been care-fully set up with different European corporations. The consequences of this cancelled trip are immense. To mention a few: lost business, daily currency and economic changes that may affect business contracts, delayed and missed opportunities that may not be rescheduled.

As such, I believe that you should compensate me for their failure to provide competent customer service. As it is impossible to put a price on the loss of my time and the inconvenience incurred by the need to reschedule this entire set of meetings, I would suggest that you should award me with sufficient additional air miles to pay for these two tickets that your staff have failed to secure for me.

Please don't hesitate to contact me should you require any additional details.

Sincerely

Dr. Phil Evans

To conclude this chapter I would like to confront you with some difficult problems and then point out possible solutions.

❏ 1.   You are the manager of a gym. One customer has a problem with body odor and people are complaining. How can you tell him about the problem without offending him?

❏ 2.   You are standing in express checkout line that says "Maximum 12 Items." The person in front of you has a chariot full of merchandise. How do you react?

❏ 3.   You have to criticize an employee but can't afford to lose him. How can you get him to accept your critique graciously?

❏ 4.   You made a reservation for 12 people for brunch on Mother's Day. When you arrive at the restaurant they give you two tables in different parts of the restaurant. What should you do?

❏ 5.   Guests are coming tonight and you want to bake a cake, but you have run out of eggs and the closest convenience store is closed for remodeling. What do you do?

Here are some possible solutions:

❏ 1.   You have several possibilities. The one that I would probably choose is the direct approach, but the man might be offended. A more elegant solution is to mail him a friendly letter and make it appear as a general reminder that is sent to all the members, saying that the warm weather is here, be sure to use deodorant, etc. If this doesn't work, you can still talk to him discreetly one-on-one, and now you have the excuse that you are following up on the letter.

❑ 2.	My suggestion: Don't react at all. I wouldn't let my day be ruined because of someone who has bad manners. I would give him the benefit of the doubt and assume that he has a reason to behave in the way he does.

❑ 3.	Do not react in anger. Prepare yourself adequately. Find a time when he is receptive and talk to him one-on-one. Don't just offer criticism but acknowledge the things he does well. Try to criticize the situation, not the person.

❑ 4.	Talk to the person in charge and, with persistence but without anger, point out that they accepted a reservation for 12 people at one table. Tell them that two tables are unacceptable and that you refuse to be seated at them. Don't give up. Insist that their commitment be honored. Don't sit down until they provide an acceptable seating arrangement. You will get your table.

❑ 5.	You could go to the closest restaurant and talk to the manager or chef. Using the magic words, "Could you help me, please?" tell him your predicament and ask if you could buy two dozen eggs from him. He will most likely say yes.

Now that we have seen several successful strategies that get you to yes, it is time for you to work on your own style and tackle your own negotiations. Remember to plan ahead using the techniques we have covered. The checklist in the next chapter will be of additional help to keep your actions on the right track.

Chapter 16

A checklist

This checklist will help you verify that you have taken everything into account before setting in motion your plan to get what you want. During your campaign use the checklist to see that all is going according to plan.

Before negotiations, ask yourself:

❑ 1.   Do I know what I want to achieve? Have I defined my maximum and minimum goals?

❑ 2.   Do I have enough information about the person or company I'm dealing with? Is he or she the appropriate negotiating partner? Do I know enough about his or her negotiating strategy, age, position, influence? Have these details been corroborated?

❑ 3.   Do I have enough information about the background, the line of business, the practices, the locality? Have these details been corroborated?

❏ 4.   Am I familiar down to the last detail with the actual business that is under negotiation? Am I well-versed in the objective and subjective aspects of the case?

❏ 5.   Are there personality clashes involved? If so, can these be cleared up beforehand? What is the general atmosphere? Do I have to take steps to improve it?

During negotiations ask yourself:

❏ 6.   Do I feel at ease or do I need to make changes? Seating arrangements, glare from the sun, etc.

❏ 7.   Have I established my relationship with the other party? Do I have a clear idea of the personalities of those involved? Have I identified the leader?

❏ 8.   Do I have my eyes and ears open?

❏ 9.   Is the relationship with the other party changing in some way?

❏ 10.   Who is running the meeting? Do I need to take back control?

❏ 11.   Am I still keeping my eyes and ears open? Is the relationship with the other party still satisfactory?

After negotiations ask yourself:

❑ 12.   Debriefing: what mistakes or misjudgments have I made? What was the reason? What could I have done better?

Dear Reader,

I would like to congratulate you for having worked through this book. You now have a firm foundation for getting what you want. No longer can you be swayed by strong opponents. This book will help you to develop self-confidence and become more assertive.

I am often asked whether this is a business or self-help book, and my answer is always the same: It is both. To be successful, you have to be able to communicate effectively. And once you have that skill, you'll find that it is equally useful in your business and personal life.

Now that you have the power to get what you want without hurting others, I urge you to use your newly acquired skills with responsibility and consideration.

I wish you good luck!

Bruno Gideon

P.S. You'll find additional information and other readers' experiences on my Website,

www.brunogideon.com